An Illustrated History of Maine

Neil Rolde

Charles C. Calhoun
Illustrations Editor

Published by the Friends of the Maine State Museum
To Commemorate the 175th Anniversary of Statehood

Augusta, Maine

1995

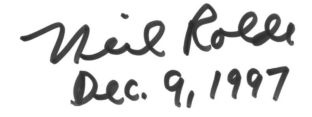

Neil Rolde
Dec. 9, 1997

To John G. Morse, Jr.
1918-1993

Lumberman, businessman, publisher, philanthropist,
who loved Maine history

cover: (detail) Fitz Hugh Lane, *Camden Mountains from
the South Entrance to the Harbor*, 1859.

frontispiece: Maine State Seal, mid-19th century.
Oil on linen. Signed E. W. Parkhurst, Gardiner.

Library of Congress Catalog Card Number 95-61976
ISBN: 0-913764-26-4

FIRST EDITION

Designed by Mahan Graphics, Bath, Maine
Printed by J.S. McCarthy Company, Augusta, Maine

The purpose of the Friends of the Maine State Museum is to benefit the Museum
and its mission to preserve Maine's heritage. The Friends benefit the Museum
through the development and implementation of volunteer support, educational
programs, fundraising, acquisition and management of real property, publications,
and promotion of the Museum. For information on membership in the Friends or
on the Maine State Museum, contact the Friends of the Maine State Museum,
State House Station # 83, Augusta, Maine 04333-0083. (207) 287-2304.

Foreword

MAINE IS A VERY SPECIAL PLACE. This new illustrated history of our state should prove enjoyable to people who love it, as well as to those learning about it for the first time.

Readers who know Maine will be reminded of the natural beauty, the struggle for survival, the ingenuity and artistry, the amusements, and the ongoing attempts to build a better life that each generation of Maine people has experienced.

Those new to Maine, including our children, have perhaps the most to gain from this richly visual introduction to the fascinating history of our state. Everyone will find something new in the results of recent research and in the artifacts collected from throughout the state by the Maine State Museum.

The thousands of Maine people with whom I have worked during my legal, journalistic, and business careers, and now as Governor, have given me a deep appreciation of all that our state is and all that it can become.

The publication of *An Illustrated History of Maine* provides an excellent example of this: a non-profit volunteer organization established to support an educational agency of state government has produced a beautiful volume made possible by the personal generosity of Maine business woman Elizabeth Noyce and the donated authorship of popular historian Neil Rolde. Artifacts pictured from the Maine State Museum collections represent gifts from people throughout the state as do illustrations from other Maine institutions. The hard work of many other individuals and several local companies complete this complex cooperative project. Such cooperative efforts have built our state and will continue to enhance it in the future. My thanks to those whose efforts have brought us this extraordinary volume—and my best wishes to its readers.

ANGUS S. KING, JR., *Governor*

INTRODUCTION

An ILLUSTRATION CAN BE A PICTURE OR DIAGRAM intended to make something easier to understand. An historical example or incident can serve the same purpose. *An Illustrated History of Maine* is intended to make the story of Maine's beginnings easier to understand and more accessible to a larger audience. It briefly outlines Maine's history through a collection of illustrations both graphic and textual. Neil Rolde's storytelling skills have produced a highly readable history of the state populated with interesting individuals and exciting incidents. Illustrations editor Charles Calhoun and the Maine State Museum staff members have supplemented the text with rich visual images which present the works of nature, prehistoric toolmakers, map makers, photographers, manufacturers, craft workers, and artists of many specialties. Althogther, these offer something of the essence of each period of Maine's history, not simply the facts and figures.

The Maine State Museum is a branch of state government which conducts research and develops organized collections of scientific specimens and cultural artifacts representing the full spectrum of Maine's natural and human history. Using this physical evidence, the Museum educates the public about this history through exhibits, lectures, and presentations, and various publications. The Friends of the Maine State Museum, a non-profit organization, was recently established to support the Museum's mission through voluntary citizen action. This book is a result of that support.

Whether you already know a lot about Maine, or wish to start learning, this book will be valuable to you. The Maine State Museum and Friends are pleased to introduce you to a book which we feel will contain something new for everyone initially, and which will also serve as an enjoyable review whenever you pick it up again.

JOSEPH R. PHILLIPS
Director, Maine State Museum
Trustee, Friends of the Maine State Museum

1.1

MAINE IN PREHISTORY

❧ THE BEDROCK

ETERNAL MAINE...land of the white pine...a jagged coastline awash with spume...evergreen-studded islands amid cobalt bays...a necklace of sparkling lakes and ponds dotting forests as far as the eye can see...western mountains...blueberry barrens. Maine's natural environment presents timeless images. A northern climate, cold waters, snow, stony ground, colorful fall leaves add to the pattern. Here is bedrock Maine, the stage against which all of our history has been played.

Far in the northwest corner of Maine, in a region next to the Quebec border called the Chain Lakes Massif, the earliest rocks have been found, one and a half billion years old. The story they tell reads like science fiction: continents colliding, volcanos erupting, a fused Europe/Africa separating from North America. At one time, Maine had coral growing in its seas. Then, ice was everywhere. The last glaciers flowed south from Canada 25,000 years ago, covering everything to the thickness of a mile. When they receded 15,000 years later, the earth elastically rebounded from the diminished weight; tundra eventually gave way to trees and dense woods; streams flowed, creating marshes, peat bogs, ponds, lakes, and rivers. The physical setting of present-day Maine awaited its first inhabitants.

Other terrestrial animals preceded the humans. Some of them can no longer be found among Maine's fauna. Indeed, a few are extinct, some within the memory of humans, such as the penguinish great auk, a goose-sized bird last glimpsed in 1844. Others became lost during the dimness of time long past. The woolly mammoth, for example, was a shaggy, cumbersome pachyderm with curled tusks whose presence perhaps is recorded in local Indian legends that speak of ivory-tipped arrows. More tangibly, the well-preserved bones of a specimen have recently been found in the state and are being excavated by researchers from the Maine State Museum. Other creatures, common elsewhere, have disappeared. The timber rattlesnake is gone but not regretted. Feelings toward the wolves whose howls

❧

1.1 *Artist Philip Paratore's depiction of life on the tundra, some 10,000 to 11,000 years ago, in the Magalloway River Valley of northwestern Maine. The ancient circle of rocks incorporated into the modern diorama was used by Paleo-Indian hunters to hide caches of caribou meat.*

formerly filled the night are more ambivalent. People even talk of trying to bring them back. With the caribou, also vanished, two extensive attempts at restoration have already been made, both in vain. The great herds, akin to those now roaming Labrador and similar far northern climes, were a seemingly permanent feature of Maine landscapes from the dawn of the first habitation until the modern age.

∾ THE PEOPLE OF THE DAWN

Hunting of those caribou began in Maine sometime between 11,000 and 10,000 years ago. The experts aren't quite sure when the Paleo-Indians arrived, except that they were no doubt part of the larger migration of late Ice Age *Homo sapiens* into North America. These most ancient ancestors of present-day Maine native Americans left behind the earliest known example of human construction in the state—a small circle of rocks built as a meat cache, discovered in the Magalloway River Valley and now on exhibit at the Maine State Museum. Also unearthed have been their "killing grounds" in Oxford County where throngs of caribou were stampeded into the trap of a river ford that ran red with blood, and the colorful rock mines in Penobscot County where they chipped out *chert* for arrowheads and skinning knives.

Paleo means "old" in Greek and the culture of these first inhabitants was replaced in time by other groupings of native Americans for whom the specialists have a plethora of names. The so-called "Red Paint People," who buried their dead with quantities of red ochre dye, are the best known, having been popularized by Warren K. Moorehead, a flamboyant, self-taught archaeologist who promoted them as a "lost" civilization. It was more likely they were a burial cult. But Moorehead's name has stayed anchored to one of the technical classifications of the varied prehistoric cultures of Maine—the *Moorehead Phase of the Laurentian Tradition*, so-titled because of the links of its denizens to the St. Lawrence Valley to the North.

1.2 *A vertebra which once supported the head of a young, probably eight-foot-high, woolly mammoth, which lived more than 10,000 years ago in the Scarborough area.*

1.2

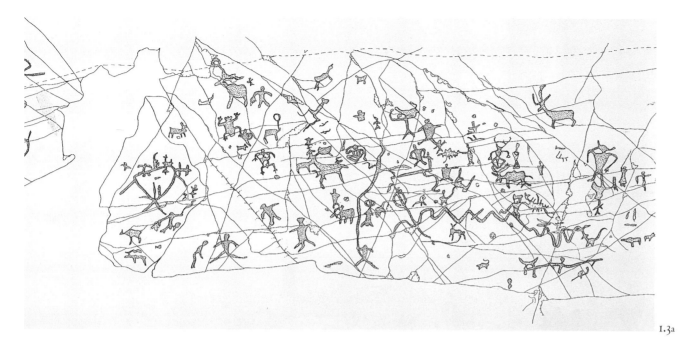

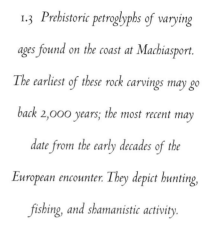

1.3 *Prehistoric petroglyphs of varying ages found on the coast at Machiasport. The earliest of these rock carvings may go back 2,000 years; the most recent may date from the early decades of the European encounter. They depict hunting, fishing, and shamanistic activity.*

1.3a

1.3b

1.4 *Paleo-Indian artifacts from the Vail Site, Aziscohos Lake basin, northwestern Maine. Made between about 11,000 and 9,000 years ago, these chert objects include projectile points used in hunting and various tools used for scraping, drilling, and engraving.*

1.4

The contents of shell middens and the survival of hand-hewn tools and weapons are the primary clues to these different peoples. One style of life, the *Susquehanna Tradition*, produced beautifully sculpted stone bowls. Pottery made of baked clay came into use more than 2,500 years ago, giving birth to the Ceramic Period. Remnants of swordfish bills found amid their mounds of debris told of a seafaring tradition.

Some were strictly hunters and gatherers. Others—those living west of the Kennebec—eventually practiced agriculture as well growing corn, beans, squash and tobacco. They brewed tea out of hemlock needles, supplying themselves instinctively with vitamin C to ward off scurvy. They manufactured bark canoes, constructed teepees of poles and skins, and wove baskets from strips of pounded willow. By the time visitors arrived from overseas, a complex society had developed.

Indeed, they were part of a much larger culture linked by trade routes as far south as Pennsylvania, as far west as the Great Lakes and as far north as Labrador.

Their languages belonged to the Algonquian family of tongues and their name for themselves was "Wabanakiak"—people of the dawn—often shortened to Abenaki or Abnaki. They considered themselves children of Gluskap, who was not exactly a God but more of a primordial hero-giant, the creator of the four seasons once the ice of the glacier had receded and who, in their mythology, still exists, holed up in a cave, chipping arrowheads for the day his people will drive out the European invaders.

Separate tribes developed in specific locations before these intruders appeared. A number of them that existed historically, like the Sokokis or the Norridgewocks or Kennebecs have entirely vanished while a few remain to this day, primarily the Penobscots and Passamaquoddies, but also bands of Malecites and Micmacs whose main territory is in Canada.

1.5

∾

1.5 *An early 20th-century Native American depiction on birch-bark of the adventures of the mythical Wabanaki founder-hero, Gluskap (or Koluskap), seen here in disguise in a canoe with Grandmother Woodchuck. The work of the Passamaquoddy artist Tomah Joseph, it illustrates an "origin story" in which Gluskap travels in a stone canoe across the sea to tell Europeans about America.*

1.7a

1.6

1.6 Discovered in a midden at Brooklin, Maine, this 11th-century Norse silver penny is evidence of the extensive trading practices of the region's native peoples. It had been exchanged with a more northerly people who had come into contact with the Vikings.

❧ THE NORSE COIN

In 1979, a minor sensation was created when a collection of Indian artifacts at the Maine State Museum was found to contain a rare and authentic Norse coin. Was this proof that the Vikings had been to Maine, since the coin had been originally found in Hancock County? Had Leif Ericsson's fabled Vinland been located downeast?

Maine archaeologists soon developed a less romantic theory of how this bit of blackened metal—a penny from the reign of King Olav Kyrre, 1066-1093—had ended up at a site on Blue Hill Bay. They saw it as an item of trade used by the Indian peoples farther north, where a Viking settlement has been located in Newfoundland, when they ventured south to Maine. The tiny coin, nevertheless, is one of the most fascinating items in the Maine State Museum's collections.

1.7b

1.7a *(facing page) The Maine State Museum's archaeological excavations at the Turner Farm Site on North Haven Island have demonstrated the variety of information about diet and fishing practices that can be gathered from a prehistoric shell midden, or shell heap. This accumulation of shells, bones, and other debris dates from 5,000 to 400 years ago.*

1.7b *A portion of the Turner Farm Site has been reconstructed in the Museum's "12,000 Years in Maine" exhibit to show how archaeologists interpret the stratification, or layering, of such deposits.*

THE EUROPEAN ENCOUNTER

∾ EARLY EXPLORATION

THE FIRST WAS JOHN CABOT, or rather Giovanni Caboto, a citizen of Venice, born in Genoa, sailing for the British king, Henry VII, who reached either Newfoundland or Cape Breton, Nova Scotia, in 1497, an epic voyage upon which all subsequent claims by England to North America were based. It was the same year in which the Portuguese explorer Vasco da Gama rounded the Cape of Good Hope and opened India and the rest of Asia to European trade.

North America, less valued than the spice and silk entrepôts of the East Indies, was probed sporadically by other visitors throughout the 1500's. Some, like Estevao Gomes, a Portuguese sailing for Spain, left an enduring trace in Maine in the names he bestowed on various physical features: i.e., Casco Bay, because of its helmet (*casco*) shape or the Bay of Fundy, originally *Bahia Profundo*, "Deep Bay." Giovanni Verrazzano, an Italian hired by the French, met open hostility from the Indians on the Maine coast when he sent an armed party ashore in 1524. Sir Humphrey Gilbert, the half-brother of Sir Walter Raleigh, reasserted England's claim in 1583, taking possession of Newfoundland, but he drowned on his return voyage home. Some 20 years later, his son Bartholomew Gilbert was aboard a ship that landed in Maine near Cape Elizabeth and farther south off York met a sailboat-load of natives. The chief was dressed in "a waistcoast of black work, a pair of breeches, cloth stockings, shoes, hat and band." As the 17th-century dawned, European influence was clearly already being felt.

A Protestant and a Catholic, both French, led an expedition to Maine in 1604 that stayed at least for the length of a northern winter. The Sieur de Monts was a Huguenot nobleman, a close friend of King Henri IV who was trying to keep his realm from splitting apart over religious differences, while Samuel de Champlain, the voyage's navigator was a devout but not intolerant Catholic. The site of their settlement was an island in the St. Croix River, not far from the modern city of Calais.

∾

2.1 *Map of the "Province of Mayne", c. 1653. This is a late 19th-century copy commissioned by the Maine antiquarian James Phinney Baxter of a 17th-century British Admiralty map of the northern New England coast.*

2.2

2.2 Giacomo Gastaldi's La Nuova Francia, *Venice, 1556. This woodcut, the first printed map devoted to New England, was based on the voyages of Verrazzano and Cartier. It includes the mythical Norumbega, a fabled land of great riches thought by later explorers to be in the Penobscot River valley.*

The settlement was not a success. The Europeans were not prepared for the rigors of the climate, temperatures reportedly so low that all liquid except their Spanish sherry froze. Even worse was the problem of scurvy, a fatal disease caused by a lack of vitamin C that killed about half of the 79 men on the island. With spring, this unpromising location was abandoned. Ironically, Champlain headed them south, past much more desirable landfalls, including Boston, Plymouth Harbor and Cape Cod, not yet settled by the English. But rather than stake their claim in these milder climes, the French returned to the north, and De Monts established his headquarters at Port Royal on the upper shore of Nova Scotia.

A year later, an incident along the Maine coast profoundly influenced future English colonization. A ship's captain named George Weymouth kidnapped five Indians—according to popular tradition, by luring them aboard his vessel by promising them a bowl of green peas, and then sailing off. Some of the captives were lodged in Plymouth, England with the commander of the fort there, Sir Ferdinando Gorges. The others stayed in London with the Chief Justice, Sir John Popham. Gorges and Popham, inspired by the glowing stories their "guests" told about America, became prime movers in the efforts to settle this new world.

Forming joint stock companies in 1606, they sent out ships to the land now known as Virginia in honor of Queen Elizabeth. In 1607, a party of English reached Jamestown in South Virginia. That same month of May, a similar group of "planters" set sail for Maine.

Like the French at St. Croix, these would-be settlers did not tarry long. They set up camp on Popham Beach, at the mouth of the Kennebec, held a service of thanksgiving, built the first American ship—a 30-ton pinnace, the VIRGINIA—lasted out the winter, but then lost their leaders, George Popham to death at the age of 58, and Raleigh Gilbert to the need to assume his place as head of his family once his older brother had died. The remaining colonists packed up, took the *Virginia* with them, and went home to England.

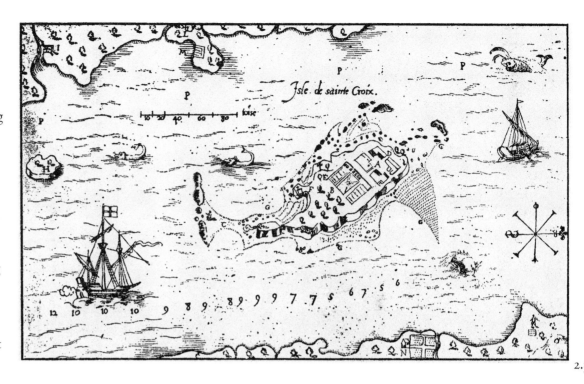

2.3

᙮

2.3 *Champlain probably drew this map of the island he colonized in 1604 in the St. Croix River after returning to France, and the details of the island's houses and gardens may be fanciful. The actual St. Croix settlement barely survived its first harsh winter and was quickly abandoned.*

2.4 *The Dutch landscape painter Gerard van Edema was brought to North America in the 1690s to depict the New World for his English patrons. This fishing station he recorded at Placentia Bay, Newfoundland, closely resembles similar seasonal encampments along the Maine coast at that time. As the historian D. W. Meinig writes, it "needs only a drizzle of rain and the stench of rotting fish guts to seem fully authentic."*

2.4

∽ THE SEEDS OF WAR

The next important French expedition to Maine reflected the dominant position of the church of Rome in 17th-century France. Its patron, the Marquise de Guercheville, had strong ties to the Jesuits and bankrolled an attempt to create a colony where the members of this priestly order would be in charge. The Marquise's colony was originally slated for Kadesquit, a site near Bangor. Instead, the ship carrying Father Pierre Biard and other religious figures landed near the mouth of Somes Sound, on Mount Desert Island, where the settlement they began to erect was named Saint Sauveur.

Yet hardly had the French settled in when a sailing vessel unexpectedly appeared offshore. It was soon discerned to be an English warship. Father Biard has described how it: "…sped forward faster than a dart, having wind to spare, all decked out in red, the flags of England flapping, the trumpets and two drums joining the racket."

The French were under attack. Musketeers on board opened fire. The French captain ordered his crew to respond. One of the priests, manning a cannon, was cut down by a rifle ball in the chest. Within minutes, the fight was over, the rest of the French taken prisoner.

Leading the assault was Captain Samuel Argall, who had cruised north from Jamestown with orders to "dislodge" any French settlements he discovered on land then claimed by England, essentially the entire Atlantic coast. Not only was Saint Sauveur demolished but also Port Royal, the French base in Nova Scotia. The prisoners, after various adventures, finally were returned to France.

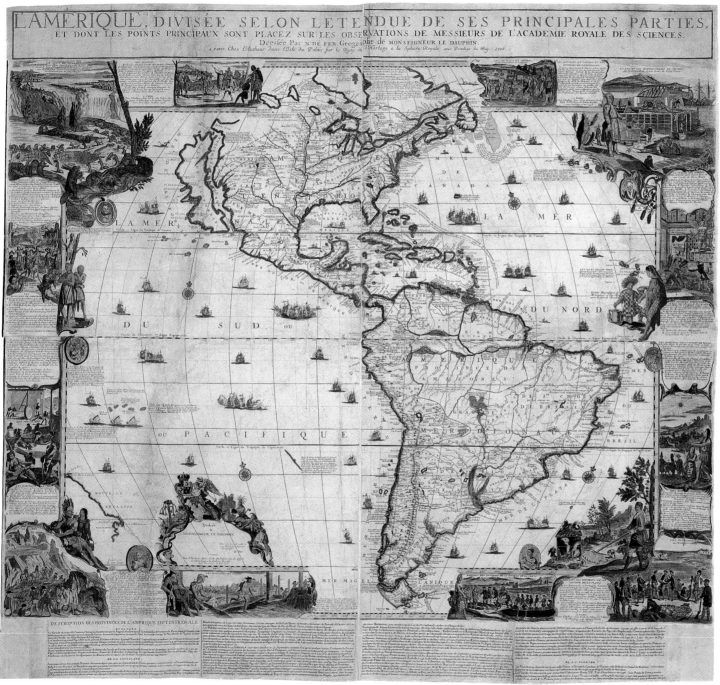

2.5 Nicolas de Fer's L'Amérique, divisée selon L'Etendu de ses Principales Parties, *Paris, 1705. The vignette in the upper right depicts fishermen drying cod on the North Atlantic coast—the chief activity that first attracted Europeans to the Gulf of Maine. Timber, furs, and land speculation inspired further exploration.*

2.5

NEW ENGLAND

The most remarqueable parts thus named.
by the high and mighty Prince CHARLES,
nowe King of great Britaine

THE PORTRAICTUER OF CAPTAYNE IOHN SMITH ADMIRALL OF NEW ENGLAND.

Ætat.37. A°1616

These are the Lines that shew thy Face; but those
That shew thy Grace and Glory, brighter bee:
Thy Faire-Discoueries and Fowle-Overthrowes
Of Salvages, much Civilliz'd by thee
Best shew thy Spirit; and to it Glory Wyn,
So, thou art Brasse without, but Golde within.

If so, in Brasse (too soft Smiths Acts to beare)
I fix thy Fame, to make Brasse Steele out weare.
Thine, as thou art Virtues,
John Dauies. Heref:

Simon Passeus sculpsit

COGNITA MIHI
VIENS IN SERVIET

A Scale of Leagues
Observed and described by Captayn John Smith
1614

London
Printed by James Reeue

Place names on map: Aborden, Gunnells, Lowmonds, Edenborough, Cambridg, St Iohn Towne, Norwich, Fines Ils, The Base, The River forth, Prewins, Pembrocks Bay, Schooters hill, Leth, Marthes Ile, Sandwich, Highton Ils, Gerrards Ils, Dartmouth, Barty Ils, Willowby Ils, Harrington Bay, Cape Elizabeth, Pegwin Pt, Ipswich, P. Kent, Snadoun hill, P Bristo, Beston, Hull, Poynt Gnave, Smithe Iles, SouthHampton, Cape Anna, P Mishoppe, Bristow, Basable, Salem, Talbotts Bay, Fawmouth, Frauncis Ile, The River CHARLES, Charlton, Claiborns Ils, Cheuyot hills, P Saltonstale, London, Oxford, Poynt Suttliff, Poynt Gorge, Cape IAMES, NEW Plimouth, P. Standish, Milford, We. Bay, STUARDS Bay, Barwick

Simon Passeus sculpsit

2.6

There, on the coast of Maine, facing what is today Acadia National Park, in one of the most scenic spots in the world, a brief exchange of gunfire planted the bloody seeds of a century and a half of war.

In Maine, after the battle of Saint Sauveur, the English had the field to themselves. One of the less stressed facts in American history school texts is that the Pilgrim fathers financially sustained their colony at Plymouth with the furs they traded at their outpost near Augusta on the Kennebec River. They had been in Maine since 1625 when they sent Edward Winslow north with a boatload of corn that he exchanged for 700 pounds of beaver pelts. Between 1631 and 1636, the Pilgrims shipped more than six tons of valuable fur to London.

Their little commercial settlement was also the site of the first recorded murders of Europeans to take place in Maine. A ship's captain named John Hocking, an agent for two British lords who had claims on the Kennebec territory, while attempting to intrude on the Plymouth colony's monopoly, shot one of a pair of Pilgrims trying to cut his vessel's cables. The man's companion fired back and killed Hocking.

But not only Pilgrims came to Maine. While thousands of Puritans poured into Massachusetts, the land to the north of the Piscataqua River had been granted to Sir Ferdinando Gorges, an ardent Royalist and Anglican who had no sympathy for dissenters from the established religion. Maine, in effect, became a rival center of power for those who opposed the Calvinists who controlled the Massachusetts Bay Colony to the south.

Gorges intended to establish the capital of his "Province of Maine"—an area that also included the northern Isles of Shoals, Nantucket, and Martha's Vineyard—at a location on the coast originally called Agamenticus, but later known as Gorgeana. Today, it is the town of York. His plans for the community, where he intended to reside in a manor house as the Lord Proprietor, were appropriately ambitious and feudal in tone. Gorgeana was to be a city, an English market center with a cathedral as the seat of an Anglican bishop, a mayor, 12 aldermen, 24 councilmen, two to four "Sergeants of the White Rod," two courts, and the like. The manor house did get built, but Sir Ferdinando never crossed the Atlantic to reside in it. The English Civil War, breaking out in 1642, kept him at home. Nor did

2.6 John Smith, "New England Observed...", London, 1624. Captain Smith's highly detailed map gave "New England" its name, although many of his other place names—chosen to flatter his patrons and to "anglicize" the wilderness—did not catch on. The map, which went through many editions, was designed to lure settlers and investors. The Pilgrims used an earlier version of it in 1620.

2.7

the tiny settlement in the wilderness ever fulfill his grandiose blue-print. By the time the Massachusetts Puritans took it over in 1652 and turned it into a "town," with a Board of Selectmen and Town Meeting, it was still a rough frontier opening amid the endless forest.

All along the coast of southern Maine, an "armigerous gentry" who were "loyal to their King and faithful to their church" provided a buffer to the Congregationalists farther south. Men such as Edward Godfrey at York, Alexander Shapleigh at Kittery, Richard Bonython at Saco, Robert Trelawney at Cape Elizabeth, and Henry Josselyn at Black Point (Scarborough) were leaders in the effort to create a unified government for the slowly growing Province of Maine.

The writings of John Josselyn, brother of the Scarborough squire, have left an enduring portrait of those days. The region from Winter Harbor (Biddeford Pool) to Saco is described as "one scattering town of large extent, well-stored with cattle, arable land and marshes and a saw mill" and his presentations of the animal life, like a "great and grim overgrown she-wolf" and rattlesnakes nine feet long have earned him the title of Maine's first naturalist. Josselyn is also Maine's first teller of tall tales. His fauna also included "sea serpents" and "mermen." An enduring part of Maine folklore is his narration of what happened one day to a man named Michael Mitton who was out hunting sea birds in Casco Bay. Suddenly, two scaled hands arose from the water and gripped the gunwhale of Mitton's canoe. The terrified fisherman grabbed his hatchet and chopped them off, horrifed by the geysers of purple blood as the hideous creature sank.

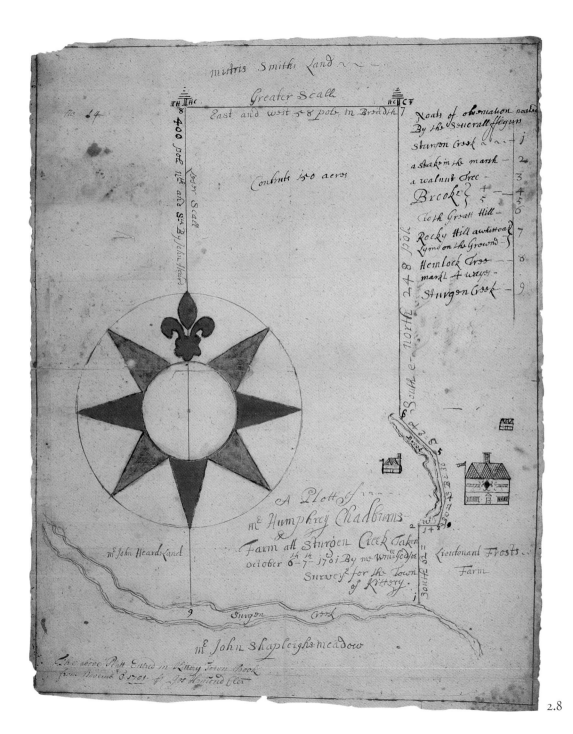

2.7 *(facing page)* "Madame Penobscot" was a Native American captured in Maine and brought back to England in the early 1600s. The "princess" was one of several captives who were taught English and used to promote colonization of New England. Her portrait in Jacobean dress now hangs at The Vyne, a country house in Hampshire, England.

2.8 Surveyor William Godsoe's "Plott of Mr Humphrey Chadburns Farm att Sturgen Creek", Kittery, 1701. The notion of turning "wilderness" into "property" was one of the dominant themes of Maine's colonial history.

2.8

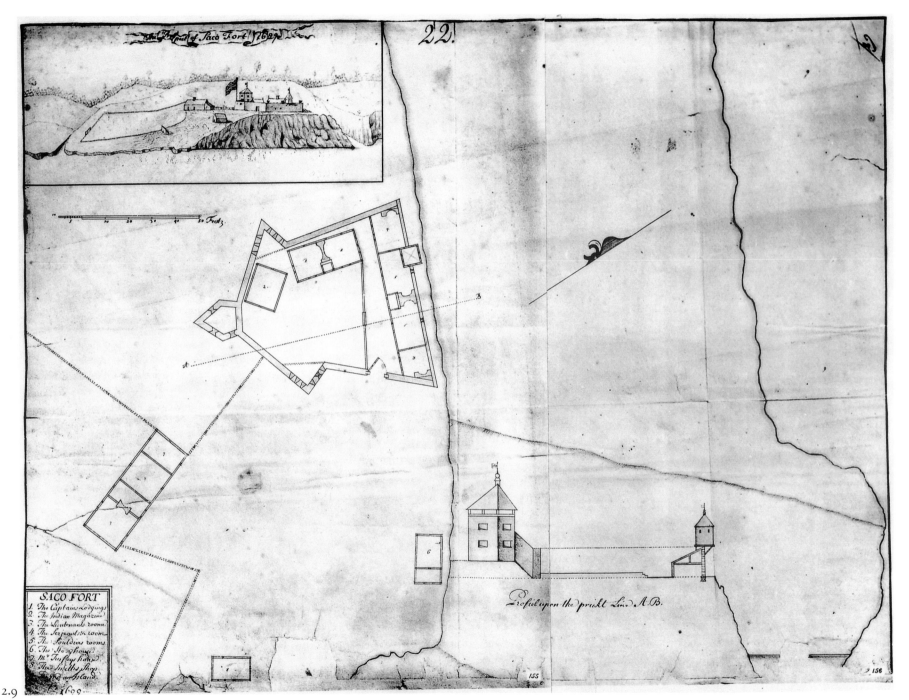

The Pourtrait of Saco Fort 1699

22

SACO FORT
1. The Captains Lodgings
2. The Indian Magazin
3. The Lieutenants room
4. The Serjeants room
5. The Souldiers rooms
6. The Hogs house
7. Mr Turfey's Barn
8. The Smiths Shop
The Fort and Island
1699

Profiel upon the prickt Line A.B.

2.9

2.10

Michael Mitton was an actual person who lived on Peaks Island. His father-in-law, George Cleeve, had received a patent of ownership from Gorges for what is now Portland and all of the islands of Casco Bay. Cleeve was continually embroiled with other settlers, particularly John Winter, agent for the Trelawney interests in the Cape Elizabeth area.

Cleeve's political machinations, his flirting with the Cromwell supporters in England, eventually led to a fracturing of the Province of Maine into four separate jurisdictions. Only three towns, Kittery, York, and Wells, were left in Maine after Cleeve broke off a "Province of Lygonia," stretching from Cape Porpoise to Cape Elizabeth. Farther north was "Sagadahoc," from the Kennebec to the Penobscot, and beyond were the French on territory deemed to be part of Maine. The stage was set in the early 1650s for a decisive political event.

∾

2.9 (facing page) The 1699 drawing by Wolfgang Romer of the British fort at Saco depicts how European military architecture was replicated in New World settings, at a time when Maine was a pawn in an international power game between Britain and France.

∾

2.10 The modern reconstruction, based on archaeological evidence, of the blockhouses and palisade fence of Fort Western (1754) at Augusta, overlooking the Kennebec. The empty area on the right is the site of the Pilgrims' Cushnoc fur-trading post of the 1620s.

2.11

2.11 *Said to have been carried on the Arnold Expedition to Quebec in 1775 but probably made at the time of the French and Indian War (1756-63), this richly carved powder horn depicts—amid its ships, sea creatures, and Indians—what may be intended to be either Quebec City or Louisbourg.*

☙ MASSACHUSETTS TAKES OVER

The date was October 23, 1651. From Boston, the governing body of the Massachusetts Bay Colony, the General Court, sent in its own words "a loving letter and friendly" to the authorities in what was left of the Province of Maine. The message: Maine is now under the jurisdiction of Massachusetts.

For some time, Governor Edward Godfrey's rump government in Kittery, York, and Wells had been aware of the expansionist tendencies of the Puritans to the south. Massachusetts forces had radiated from the center at Boston, sometimes peacefully absorbing their neighbors, sometimes employing armed might. The Pequot War of 1636 was in reality a land grab from the Indians of the southern part of the Bay Colony. Three years later, the Puritans headed north into New Hampshire, overwhelmed a group of Anglicans at Dover, and ultimately took control of Portsmouth and Exeter. An alliance in 1643, the United Colonies of New England, linked Massachusetts Bay, Plymouth, Connecticut, and New Haven for "defensive" purposes. Maine was not included because, as John Winthrop explained, "They ran a different course from us both in their ministry and civil administration." In other words, he did not recognize its legitimacy as a separate colony.

There was no response from Maine to the first "loving letter," and two more contacts in 1652 did not produce the required submission. On November 16, 1652, four Massachusetts Commissioners arrived in Kittery, accompanied by a marshall and his armed deputies.

Kittery gave in that same day. Six nights afterward, York followed suit. Within seven months, Wells had also capitulated.

But Massachusetts, now at the border of the Province of Lygonia, did not stop. Simultaneously with the surrender of Wells came the submission of Saco, Biddeford, Cape Porpoise, and Kennebunk, all theoretically under the governance of George Cleeve, who at the time was in England.

When Cleeve returned, he sought unsuccesfully to resist the Puritans. In May 1657, two of Cleeve's fellow Lygonians, Henry Josselyn in Scarborough and Robert Jordan in Cape Elizabeth, received another "loving letter and friendly." The final upshot was a meeting at Jordan's house in Spurwink, where 29 signers, among them Cleeve and Michael Mitton, bowed to Massachusetts. The date was July 13, 1658. In less than seven years, Maine had lost its independence. It would take 162 years to regain it.

2.12 *Sir William Phips (1651-95), merchant and military leader, was the first Mainer to be knighted by the British Crown.*

2.12

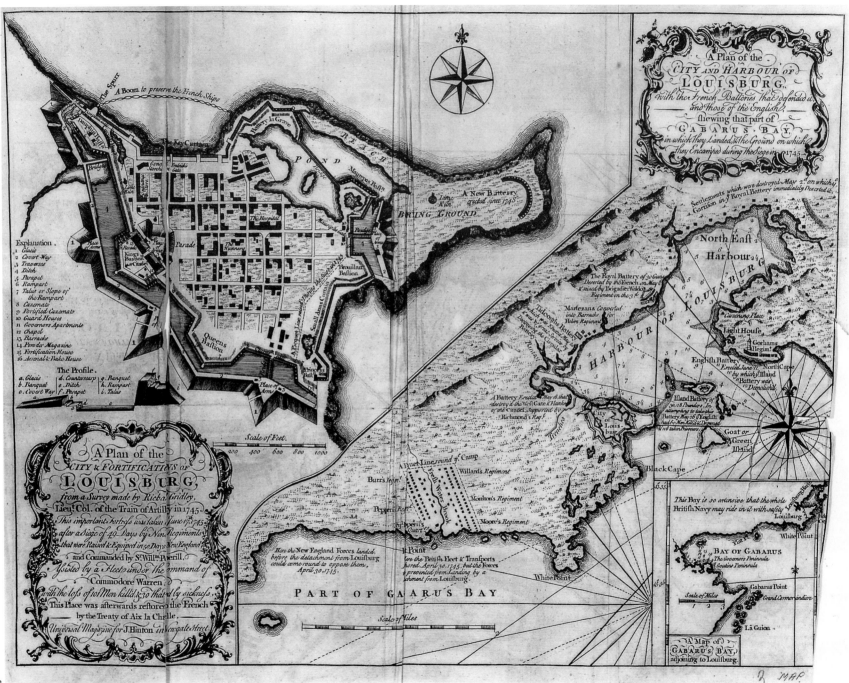

A Plan of the
CITY AND HARBOUR OF
LOUISBURG,
with the French Batteries that defended it,
and those of the English,
shewing that part of
GABARUS · BAY,
in which they Landed, & the Ground on which
they Encamped during the Siege in 1745.

A Plan of the
CITY & FORTIFICATIONS of
LOUISBURG,
from a Survey made by Richd Gridley,
Lieut. Col. of the Train of Artillery in 1745.
This important Fortress was taken June 17, 1745,
after a Siege of 49 Days by Nine Regiments
that were Raised & Equiped in 50 Days in New England,
and Commanded by Sr Willm Pepperill,
assisted by a Fleet under the Command of
Commodore Warren,
with the loss of 101 Men killd & 30 that dyd by sickness.
This Place was afterwards restored to the French
by the Treaty of Aix la Chapelle.
Universal Magazine for J. Hinton in Newgate Street.

Explanation.
1 Glacis
2 Covert-Way
3 Traverses
4 Ditch
5 Parapet
6 Rampart
7 Talus or Slope of the Rampart
8 Casemate
9 Fortified Casemats
10 Guard Houses
11 Governors Apartments
12 Chapel
13 Barracks
14 Powder Magazine
15 Fortification
16 Arsenal & Stake House

The Profile.
a. Glacis
b. Banquet
c. Covert Way
d. Countescarp
e. Ditch
f. Parapet
g. Banquet
h. Rampart
i. Talus

Scale of Feet.
200 400 600 800 1000

PART OF GABARUS BAY

HARBOUR OF LOUISBURG

North East Harbour

A Map of
GABARUS BAY,
adjoining to Louisburg.

BAY OF GABARUS
The Governors Peninsula
Goutine Peninsula

Scale of Miles

This Bay is so extensive that the whole British Navy may ride in it with safety.

❧ WAR ON THE MAINE FRONTIER

The New Englanders called him King Philip. His real name was Metacom, and he was the son of Chief Massasoit whom our schoolbooks revere as the benign friend and savior of the Pilgrims. Friction at some time between the Massachusetts Indians and the settlers in their midst was probably inevitable and finally in the summer of 1675 it erupted at Plymouth. Earlier that year, a Christian Indian named John Sassamon was found murdered. Three members of King Philip's tribe, the Wampanoags, were tried for the crime and hanged. He went to war to avenge them. The conflict was fierce

2.14

and soon spread to other parts of New England. Although Philip was hunted down and killed a year later, the fighting continued, particularly in Maine.

It was almost three months after Philip launched his first attack on Swansea, Massachusetts, that hostilities broke out on the Maine frontier. According to traditional accounts, a party of drunken English sailors was sitting on the banks of the Saco River. A canoe came by them in which sat an Indian woman with a baby. There had been a drunken discussion among the tars about the belief that Indian infants were born with an innate ability to swim. To test the theory, they deliberately upended the canoe. The baby sank, instead of darting off like a seal pup. When the frantic mother retrieved the child, it was too late. Her son, also the son of the local chief Squando, had drowned.

❧

2.13 *(facing page) The capture in 1745 of the French stronghold of Louisbourg, the "Gibraltar of the West," by forces composed chiefly of New Englanders was an important step toward increasing the colonists' sense of their own independence and military ability.*

❧

2.14 *Sir William Pepperrell (1696-1759), a wealthy Kittery landowner-soldier, led the British land forces—about a third of them from Maine—who captured Louisbourg at Cape Breton, Nova Scotia.*

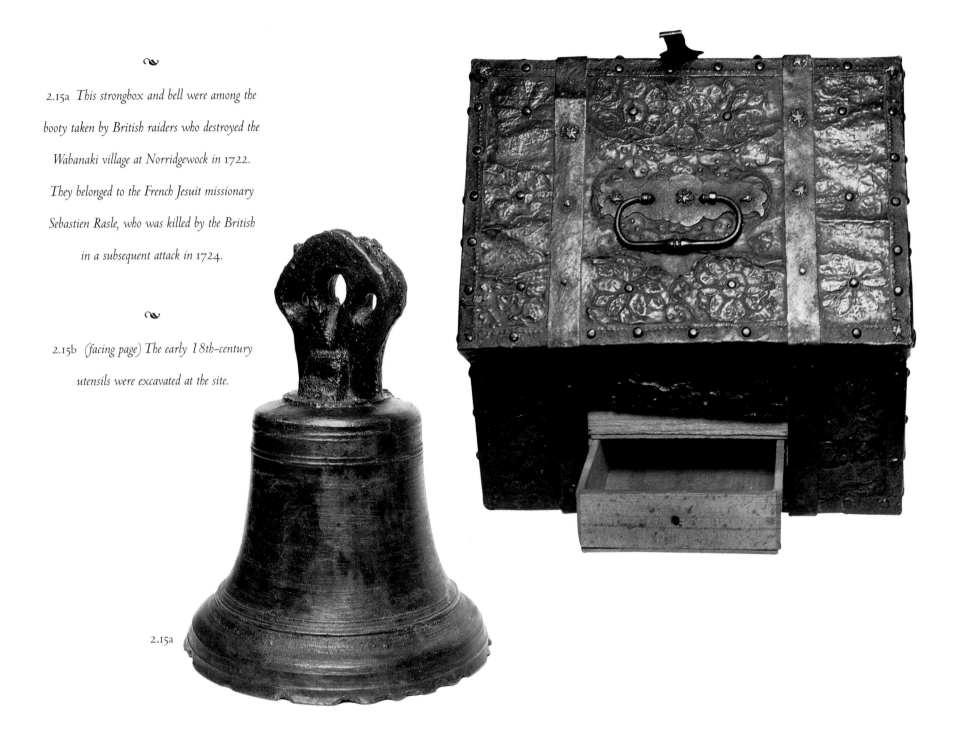

2.15a *This strongbox and bell were among the booty taken by British raiders who destroyed the Wabanaki village at Norridgewock in 1722. They belonged to the French Jesuit missionary Sebastien Rasle, who was killed by the British in a subsequent attack in 1724.*

2.15b *(facing page) The early 18th-century utensils were excavated at the site.*

2.15a

Whatever the actual cause of the hostilities, the attacks on settlers extended well beyond the Saco area. The initial raid was near Brunswick, some 40 miles to the north, and the first fatalities the English suffered were in Falmouth. The garrison forts of Saco and Scarborough were besieged, and throughout the autumn months of 1675, western Maine continued to suffer, More than 50 of the English were killed between the Piscataqua and the Kennebec.

A brief lull during the winter was followed by renewed battles. Even as Philip was being hunted down in August 1676, Indians were attacking colonists at the mouth of the Kennebec and on Arrowsic Island. In October, the local chief Mogg—Mogg Heigon, made famous in John Greenleaf Whittier's epic poem "Mogg Megone"—was routing the defenders of Scottow's Fort at Black Point, Scarborough. In another attack at the same blockhouse seven months later, a sharpshooter's bullet felled the Indian leader. Not until 1678 was a peace treaty signed, and it proved to be only temporary. This opening salvo in what turned into nearly 90 years of death and destruction on the Maine frontier cost the lives of 360 settlers east of the Piscataqua and perhaps as many as 3,000 Indians overall.

Soon, another dimension would be added. The French, contesting English hegemony in North America and elsewhere, would enter the fray. The people of the Maine, natives as well as colonizers, would become pawns in a far greater imperial struggle.

2.15b

2.16 African American slaves, usually domestic servants, were a status symbol in colonial New England. This figure is believed to represent Phyllis, the mulatto servant who accompanied Elizabeth Wendell to Falmouth (modern Portland) in 1766. Slavery was abolished in the District of Maine and Massachusetts by a court decision in 1783.

✍ A QUESTION OF OWNERSHIP

It wasn't bad enough that the English settlers in newly-expanded Massachusetts had to deal with avenging Indians and simultaneously with a drought that withered their crops; they also had to suffer the attentions of Edward Randolph.

The younger son of an impoverished landed family in Kent, and no friend of the Puritans, Randolph came to Massachusetts originally to defend the land claim of his cousin, Captain John Mason, and to report back to the powerful subcommittee of the King's Privy Council that ran colonial affairs as to what was transpiring in the Bay Colony. If, in the mischief he created for the locals he could feather his own nest financially, so much the better.

Therefore, it was not surprising that the conclusion of his scathing report to London declared that the Bay Colonists had no rights to their land or to their own government. Thus, they might be forced to buy back their land titles from agents for the King, such as Randolph, who decided to stay in the New World and make his fortune through political influence.

The legal question facing the mother country was: who owned New Hampshire and Maine? On the issue of New Hampshire, which was essentially the land granted to Captain John Mason, the Chief Justices of England ruled that it was the King's possession and would be governed as a crown colony. The rights to Maine, in the same decision, were given back to the heirs of Sir Ferdinando Gorges. But the Puritans outfoxed their tormentors. Working surreptitiously, they bought out the Gorges family for 1,250 pounds. When King Charles II, in power since 1660 and forever seeking to re-establish his royal "prerogative," heard of the transaction, he was furious but confined his ire to a vigorous protest. So Massachusetts kept its now legitimate claim to Maine.

Edward Randolph wasn't finished, however. As a reward for his efforts, he was appointed to the lucrative post of Collector of Customs for New England.

2.17 *Built in 1755 by a mast agent for the Royal Navy, the gambrel-roofed Tate House in Stroudwater, near Portland, suggests the importance of the white-pine mast trade in pre-Revolutionary Maine.*

2.17

2.18

2.18 *The Lady Pepperrell House in Kittery (1760), built for the widow of the hero of Louisbourg, is the finest 18th-century Palladian building in Maine.*

2.19 *(facing page) Samuel de Champlain produced perhaps the most beautiful 17th-century map of New France, published in his* Voyages *(Paris, 1612). The Native Americans depicted are stylized representations of the peoples he had encountered in northern New England and Maritime Canada.*

Then, he went to New York and teamed up with another Royalist named Sir Edmund Andros, who had been put in charge of a catch-all government that stretched from New Jersey to Maine. Under the Dominion of New England, as it was called, every local provincial government had been suppressed. The new King, James II, was far more autocratic than his more easy-going brother Charles and was determined to crush the Puritans. In fact, many Englishmen began to suspect that James intended to re-impose the Catholic religion on their Protestant country. These fears led to the Stuart king's downfall in a bloodless revolution in 1689.

Meanwhile, Andros, on an expedition to eastern Maine, managed to antagonize the French by pillaging the home of the Baron de Castin in the present-day town of Castine. Since the French noble-

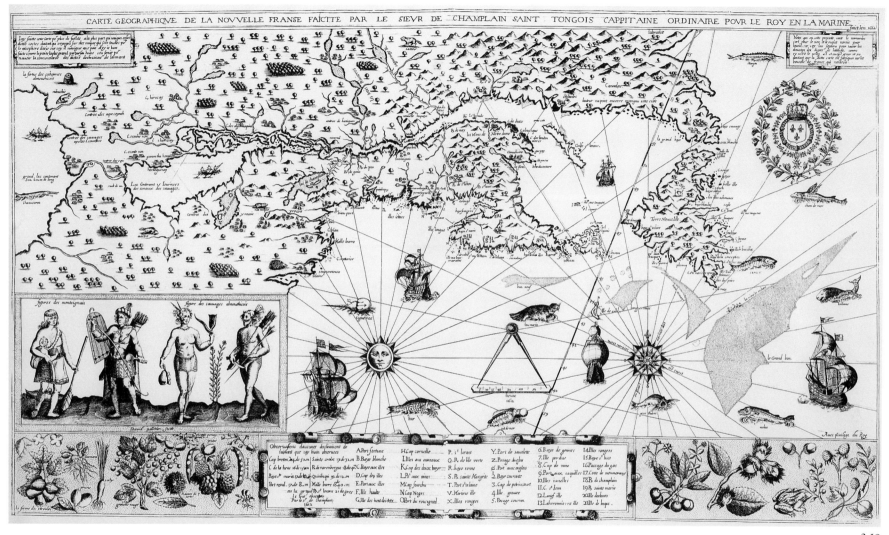

man had married the daughter of Madockawando, the powerful Penobscot chief, the result was a retaliatory raid on the fort established by Andros at Pemaquid. Once again, Maine was aflame. But by then Andros and Randolph had been driven from power and jailed in a citizens' revolt. It had followed on the news of the "Glorious Revolution" in England that had toppled James II and replaced him with his sister Mary and her husband William of Orange.

2.20 *Joseph Heath surveyed much of the Kennebec Valley for the Pejepscot Proprietors in 1719, at a time when few settlers had penetrated a region still embroiled in the wars with the French and the Indians.*

❧ THE WAR AGAINST FRANCE

A key figure of the international struggles between France and England that continued in North America after 1689 was a man born on a Woolwich, Maine, farm. The son of a carpenter, one of 26 children, arising from poverty through a combination of native talent, persistence, aggressiveness, and good luck, William Phips became the first "American" to be knighted by the British crown. The feat that earned him this distinction was his dogged determination in finding a sunken Spanish treasure in the Caribbean worth $300,000—a fabulous sum in those days. The King, grateful for the cut he received, rewarded Phips with a knighthood. After the "Glorious Revolution," Phips's political connections, particularly to the influential Boston religious leaders Increase and Cotton Mather, won him the governorship of Massachusetts.

Even earlier, Phips, a giant of a man with a fiery temper and blunt frontier ways, had been involved in the war against the French, having captured their Nova Scotian stronghold of Port Royal in 1690. As Governor, Phips sought to extend his conquests by attacking the citadel of Quebec City itself. Here, he was ignominiously defeated and had to retreat, yet without suffering too much loss of prestige and popularity. He served in the Governor's chair throughout the witchcraft hysteria at Salem and continued to run the province during the rest of King William's War, seeing Fort William Henry, the stone fortification he had built at Pemaquid, assaulted repeatedly and even captured by the French. The Treaty of Ryswick in September 1697 officially ended that phase of the Anglo-Gallic conflict (although it was two years later, at a gathering on Casco Bay, that the New World part of the fighting ended), and by then Phips was already dead. A new war—Queen Anne's—soon flared. There were battles in Maine in 1703. British troops invading Canada were more successful than in the past, capturing Port Royal again in 1710. The 1713 Treaty of Utrecht let the British retain their prize of Nova Scotia, but the French were allowed to hang onto Cape Breton Island. The fortress of Louisbourg they erected at its eastern extremity became a thorn in the side of the New Englanders, a base from which the French were continually raiding southward.

An attack on this huge redoubt occurred in 1745, led by the Kittery Point squire and merchant, William Pepperrell. It was an offensive thrust organized without the help of the British government or the British Army, financed and led by the Massachusetts Legislature, where Pepperrell was President of the Council, or upper body. At least a third of Pepperrell's men came from Maine; many were veterans of the fierce fighting that had been going on for years, which included signal victories over the French and Indians, like the devastating 1724 raid on Norridgewock—in which the famous Jesuit missionary Father Sebastien Rasle was killed—and the bloody 1725 battle of Lovewell's Pond.

Pepperrell and his rag-tag colonial army, with some help from the Royal Navy, captured the fortress of Louisbourg. The victory, coming at a time when British fortunes were low in Europe and Asia, made the Kittery merchant an instant hero. He was ennobled by the King, who created him a baronet (a form of hereditary knighthood), the first "American" ever so honored. Nonetheless, the Whig politicians in power in London handed back his conquest to the French three years later, thereby engendering an immense outpouring of ill-feeling, resentment, and mistrust of the royal government among the people of New England.

In the 1750s, new British expeditions were sent to Canada and, under competent commanders like Sir Jeffrey Amherst and General James Wolfe, successfully re-took Louisbourg and, in the end, overwhelmed Quebec City, the heart of what had once been a vast French empire in North America. The Treaty of Paris in 1763 at last brought peace, at least between the British and the French.

2.20

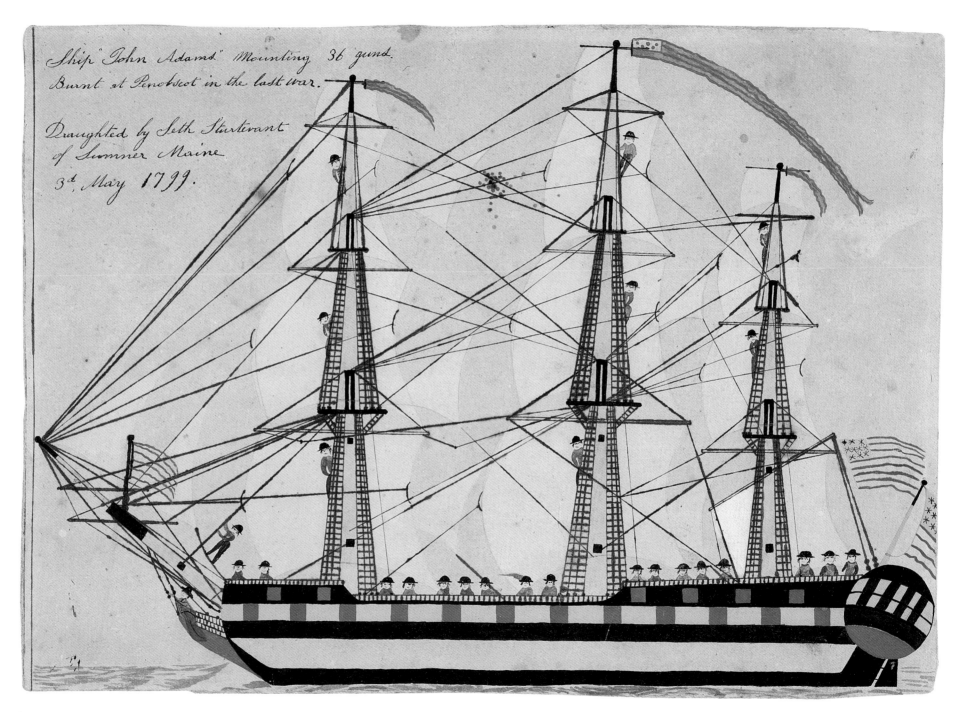

Ship "John Adams" Mounting 36 guns.
Burnt at Penobscot in the last war.

Draughted by Seth Sturtevant
of Sumner Maine
3d May 1799.

MAINE AND INDEPENDENCE

∾ PRELUDE TO REVOLUTION

ON SEPTEMBER 21, 1774, a large throng of Cumberland County residents gathered at the tavern of a Mrs. Alice Ross Greele in Falmouth (today, Portland) and listened to an unusual declaration from Sheriff William Tyng. Before the attentive crowd, some of whom were armed, the chief law officer of this county publicly swore that he had not acted "in any way whatever," nor would he, to uphold various laws recently passed by the British Parliament. Furthermore, he pledged never to enforce such laws unless the people of the county gave him their "general consent." Having listened with great satisfaction to Tyng's avowal, the assembled mob dispersed.

It was the climax to a "Convention" held to express the sentiments of the patriots of the county. Less than two weeks later, a Massachusetts-wide Congress was held at Salem, with a five-person contingent from Cumberland County and other participants from York and Lincoln counties.

What had turned them from Englishmen into Americans, determined to maintain a separate identity and, in time, a separate political existence, from the home country? Like the development of Maine, itself, throughout the early and middle years of the 18th. century, it had been really an unconscious process, undirected and unanticipated by those participating in it.

Those key triumphs over the Indians in 1724—at Norridgewock and Lovewell's Pond—had scattered the tribes and opened Maine to further penetration by settlers. At the end of King Phillip's War, the Massachusetts General Court had set aside townships to reward veterans of the fighting. "Narragansett grants," they were called, and "Canada grants" followed, after Phips's expedition against Quebec in 1690. Three current Maine towns can be directly traced to these antecedents: Narragansett #1 (Buxton), Narragansett #7 (Gorham), and Sudbury Canada (Bethel). But it took a number of years before these and other grants, particularly in the interior, filled up with settlers.

∾

3.1 *"Ship John Adams mounting 36 guns Burnt at Penobscot in the Last War. Draughted by Seth Sturdevant of Sumner, Maine, 3d May, 1799." Sturdevant, an early settler in Sumner, got the name of the vessel wrong. His painting remains, however, one of the few contemporary depictions of a naval disaster the Americans preferred to forget.*

3.2 A 1785 engraving of the "Attack of the

Rebels Upon Fort Penobscot in the Province of

New England in which their Fleet was totally

destroyed and their Army dispersed the 14th

August 1779. By an Officer present . . ."

The American fleet is shown bottled up at the

mouth of the Penobscot.

By the 1730's, the trek inland had definitely begun. Sanford was laid out in 1734, Windham in 1735, North Berwick in 1736, New Gloucester in 1737. By the 1760s, when the rate of settlement began to increase, the line stretched west to Fryeburg and Bridgton and along the coast to places like Bucksport, Gouldsborough, and Machias. Proprietors, great and small, claimed land and tried to lure families to inhabit it. New Gloucester reflected the fact that citizens of old Gloucester in Massachusetts had been offered a tract of Maine land through the General Court and had distributed it to local residents willing to settle it. In similar grass-roots fashion, New Marblehead and New Boston were created. (Today, they are the towns of Windham and Gray.) The large proprietors, on the other hand, aspired to be developers on a grandiose scale. Sir William Pepperrell developed Biddeford and Saco, which was known as Pepperrellborough for 40 years. Samuel Waldo owned even more land; out of his holdings, three Maine counties have been carved—Waldo, Knox and Lincoln. Of German origin, Waldo went to the Continent for his settlers, bringing back Rhineland Germans and French Huguenots to the mid-coast area. The Kennebec Proprietors, the Pejepscot Proprietors, and the Pemaquid Proprietors were other major landowners, usually with connections to Boston investors, who sought to "civilize" Maine's wilderness.

The process of acculturation that turned Mainers into Americans was, in part, a natural if not inevitable phenomenon. The conditions of life on the frontier were quite different from what they were in England. Violence was endemic because of the troubles with the French and Indians. The system of land tenure, derived from Massachusetts, was not as democratic as one might think but compared to British practice, it was egalitarian. True, there were great landholders in Maine, yet local attitudes toward the absentee proprietors hardly showed the hat-in-hand respect that existed in rural England. Complicating matters was the confusion over boundaries and titles to the land, in an area that had scarcely been surveyed. In the 1760s, groups of settlers (probably squatters) along the Sheepscot River donned Indian disguises and terrorized a proprietor who was threatening to evict them. "White Indians" in Woolwich burned down the houses of tenants who were collaborating too closely with another proprietor. Mob action to redress grievances was condoned throughout Massachusetts, with the infamous Boston mob taking the lead. James Cargill of Newcastle, Maine, an

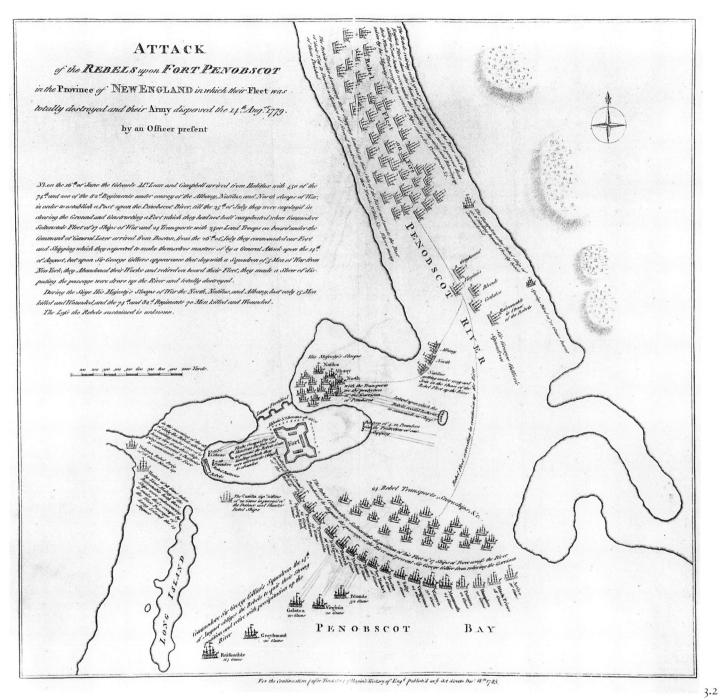

ATTACK

of the REBELS *upon* FORT PENOBSCOT

in the Province *of* NEW ENGLAND *in which their Fleet was*

totally destroyed and their Army *dispersed the 14.th Aug.st 1779.*

by an Officer present

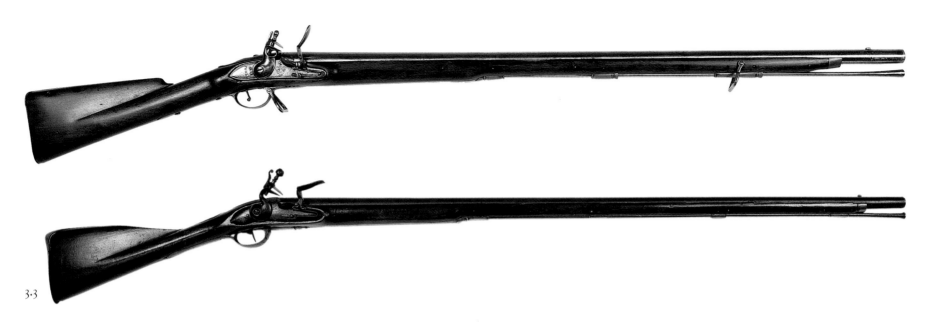

3·3

3.3 *The muskets are a British "Brown Bess" flint-lock (c. 1770) and its cruder replica, the American "Committee of Safety" flintlock (1776-80).*

3.4 *An 1814 engraving of the naval battle at Castine entitled "Sir George Colliers Victory in Penobscot Bay 1779." The failure of the patriots' flotilla to seize the fort at Castine was one of the greatest naval disasters of the American Revolution.*

Published Nov.ʸ 1, 1814, by Joyce Gold, Naval Chronicle Office, 103, Shoe Lane, London.

Baily Sculp.

Sir George Colliers victory in Penobscot Bay 1779.

1779

3·4

Indian-fighter notorious for having committed atrocities against the natives, also led a mob against three of his neighbors who displeased him. Despite his roughneck ways and his record of imprisonment for his crimes against the Indians, he was elected to town office and made a captain and a colonel in the Revolutionary militia. It seems safe to say that the statesmen in London, whose mistakes of judgment inflamed their colonial countrymen, could hardly imagine, never mind understand, the kind of society that produced a James Cargill.

When the Coercive Acts were passed with the expectation that their harshness would end the defiance of New England, it was little wonder that Maine, following upon Massachusetts, produced scenes of resistence. For example, Richard King's home in Scarborough was damaged after King was reputed to favor the Stamp Act. John Malcolm, an arrogant customs official at Wiscasset who had seized a vessel owned by local merchants, was tarred and feathered. Maine, in fact, in 1774 even had its own "tea party" at York.

A final consideration for Maine people in their relationship to the British was that the menace of the French in Canada had been removed once and for all in 1763. They had already received proof of their fighting abilities in 1745 when they had captured the massive fortress of Louisbourg, only to see it handed back to France in 1748. As long as the threat had existed, the support of the Royal Navy, which had been helpful at Louisbourg, seemed a necessity. Now, their destiny could safely be in their own hands.

∿ REVOLUTION DOWN EAST

News of the battles at Concord and Lexington reached the town of York on the night of April 19, 1775. The next day, 60 local militiamen began marching toward the fray. This was three full days before the Massachusetts Provincial Congress issued a call to raise an army of 13,600 men. Other Minutemen groups from Biddeford, Scarborough, and Falmouth were also soon tramping south. They did not all reach their destination of Cambridge because word

∾

3.5 Among the artifacts recovered in Stockton Harbor in 1972 by underwater archaeologists from the wreck of the American vessel DEFENCE *was this "stand" of unfired grapeshot.*

3.5

came that they were not needed. But this outpouring of Maine troops indicated that many people in Maine felt more loyal to Massachusetts than to Britain.

Maine's geographical position, however, put it in jeopardy. The entire coast was open to attack by the Royal Navy and British privateers operating out of Canada. Nova Scotia (New Brunswick had yet to be carved from that province) and Quebec presented the English with bases from which to stage their operations against various parts of Maine. Invasions of its territory were not long in forthcoming.

At first it seemed as if proximity to Canada might be an advantage to the rebels. The initial casualty suffered Down East by the British occurred during a naval "battle" not far from Canadian shores. The captain of a small cutter, the H.M.S. MARGARETTA, was fatally wounded in an exchange of musketry just off Machiasport. Brought ashore to Machias, the young officer expired at Burnham's Tavern, a landmark still standing. His captured ship, renamed the MACHIAS LIBERTY, was incorporated into the new navy created by the American insurrectionists.

Across the Nova Scotia line in the counties of Sunbury, Cumberland, and Kings were people of Yankee stock whose sentiments toward the mother country were identical to those of the hothead patriots in Machias who had taken on the British tars. The town of Maugerville's town meeting resolution sounded exactly like the words of resolves in Massachusetts and Maine as it declared:

> …that it is our Minds and Desire to submit ourselves
> to the government of Massachusetts Bay and that we
> are Ready with our Lives and fortunes to share with
> them the Event of the present struggle for Liberty.

That an army began to form in Machias with the idea of invading Nova Scotia and fomenting an uprising was therefore not surprising.

3.6 *The Burnham Tavern (1770), which still stands in Machias, was a center of patriot activity Down East during the Revolution. Here in 1775 was planned the daring attack in which the rebels captured the armed schooner* H.M.S. MARGARETTA, *in what is said to be the first naval engagement of the American Revolution.*

3.6

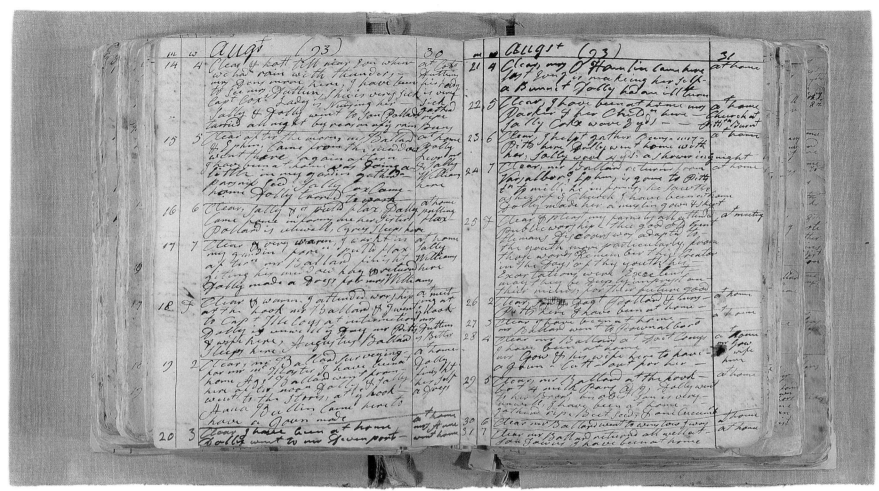

3.7 *The diary kept by the Hallowell midwife Martha Ballard in the late 18th and early 19th-century reveals aspects of the everyday world of the mid-Kennebec Valley that did not enter the official records. Like other women in her position, Ballard was at the center of the complex network of personal relationships that tied together communities on the Maine frontier. Her diary was the basis for Laurel Thatcher Ulrich's Pulitzer Prize winning history,* A Midwife's Tale *(1990), which was later made into a film.*

Before it was underway, another American invasion was actually in the field, moving upon Quebec City, where it was thought that the French Canadians, no lovers of the English, would also rise. This was the famous expedition led by Benedict Arnold that traveled up the Kennebec and Dead rivers, suffered untold hardships, and ended in ignominious defeat. The Quebeckers stayed neutral, having no more love for the Catholic-hating Yankees than they did for their British overlords. Although Montreal was captured by American general Richard Montgomery, the walls of Quebec withstood all of the American assaults until the siege was lifted and the ragged revolutionaries straggled home.

Equally quixotic was the descent upon Nova Scotia. The force under Colonel Jonathan Eddy, a Massachusetts native who had become a Nova Scotia landowner, was woefully small. Only 80 men tried to invade Fort Cumberland, a key British post. Beaten back, the Americans were soon routed by the arrival of 400 British reinforcements. All of Nova Scotia stayed loyal to the King.

But not all Nova Scotians. John Allan was the most prominent of all of the pro-American Nova Scotians and, unlike most of the others, had not come from New England. His family was Scottish, his father a regular army officer and his mother the daughter of a knight of the realm. Allan had had to flee for his life from Nova Scotia, leaving his wife and five children behind to suffer the enmity of the British authorities. George Washington's influence helped him land twin jobs as a colonel of the American infantry in charge at Machias and, more important, as the Superintendent of the Eastern Indians. Maintaining the support or at least the neutrality of the local tribes was a matter of importance to the future of the American presence in the region. The fall of Machias could imperil the entire eastern section of Maine.

3.9

~

3.8 *(facing page) "A Sketch of Mechios Mills," London, 1776 is the earliest known view of a Maine saw mill. The illustration is a vignette from a late edition of J.F. W. Des Barres'* Atlantic Neptune, *one of the most beautiful atlases ever published, much used by the Royal Navy during the Revolution.*

~

3.9 *Governor James Bowdoin II of Massachusetts (1726–90), painted by Robert Feke in 1748. A leading patriot and amateur scientist, Bowdoin was among the Boston merchants who invested heavily in Maine lands as absentee proprietors.*

3.10

3.11 (facing page) A contemporary woodcut depicting the burning of Falmouth Neck (modern Portland) by Captain Henry Mowatt of the Royal Navy in 1775. Eight hours of bombardment destroyed more than 130 dwellings and most of the warehouses, ruining the town's maritime commerce for the duration of the war.

With Indian help, a British attempt to capture Machias in August 1777 was stymied. Nor were the British ever able to dislodge Allan and his men. His difficulties in holding onto the Indians' loyalty when he lacked sufficient supplies for them—his British counterpart was trying to bribe them with ample trade goods—posed herculean problems for this patriot, one of the relatively unsung true heroes of the Revolution.

The British, however, were not entirely unsuccessful in invading Maine. Two years after they were repulsed at Machias, an amphibious operation captured Castine and the peninsula jutting into Penobscot Bay on which it sits. Quite soon, this occupied territory became a magnet for Maine and Massachusetts Tories fleeing from their former compatriots.

Some of those Loyalists had long since fled from Falmouth (Portland), Maine's largest town. A nasty incident in May 1775 had precipitated their flight. The event included the roughing up at the hands of tough militiamen of a young naval officer by the name of Mowatt—a name that would resound through the ages in Maine. Five months later, Mowatt came back with a squadron of warships and cannonaded the town, setting it afire and destroying more than 130 structures. The defenselessness of the Maine coast was never more aptly illustrated.

When the British took Castine, the authorities in Boston consequently decided that they had better strike back quickly. In less than four weeks, they assembled an armada of 19 armed vessels, sporting 344 guns, plus 24 transports carrying 1,000 soldiers. No worse American military disaster was to ensue until Pearl Harbor.

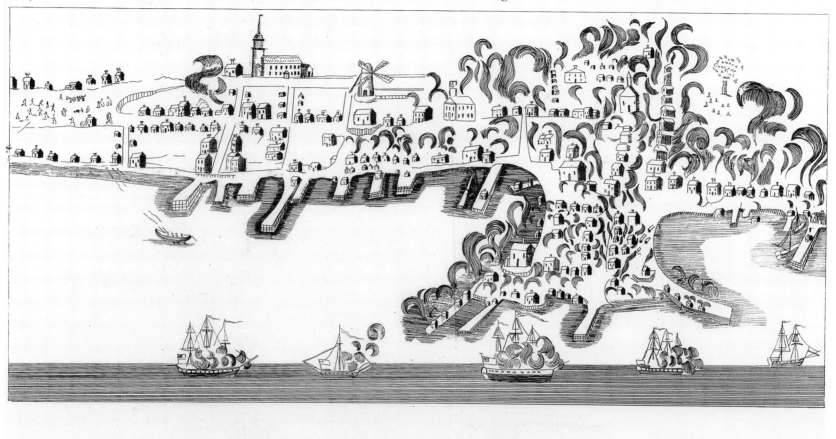

THE TOWN of FALMOUTH, *Burnt by Captain* MOET, Oct.r 18th 1775.

Facsimile from "Impartial History of the War," Vol 2, published in Boston, 1781.

3.11

3.12   *Despite their sense of remoteness, the more prosperous residents of the District of Maine emulated the style of life of Boston and Salem, as these decorative objects from the Maine State Museum's collections reveal. Below: A miniature slant-front desk of carved walnut and maple, made in Maine (1730-50) and owned by Judge Rishworth Jordan (1719-1808) of Biddeford. Right: A high chest of black walnut, birch, white pine and sumac (c. 1750-70), attributed to Samuel Sewall of York. This is one of the finest surviving examples of early formal furniture in Maine.*

3.12

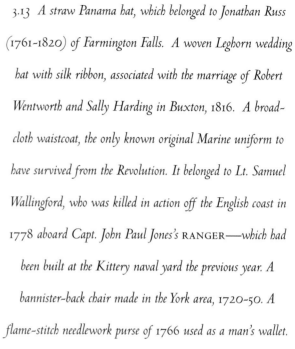

3.13 *A straw Panama hat, which belonged to Jonathan Russ (1761-1820) of Farmington Falls. A woven Leghorn wedding hat with silk ribbon, associated with the marriage of Robert Wentworth and Sally Harding in Buxton, 1816. A broadcloth waistcoat, the only known original Marine uniform to have survived from the Revolution. It belonged to Lt. Samuel Wallingford, who was killed in action off the English coast in 1778 aboard Capt. John Paul Jones's* RANGER—*which had been built at the Kittery naval yard the previous year. A bannister-back chair made in the York area, 1720-50. A flame-stitch needlework purse of 1766 used as a man's wallet.*

3.13

3.14

History lays the blame on the leadership of the expedition. So did the contemporaries of Admiral Dudley Saltonstall, a Connecticut man, who suffered a court-martial for his role in the affair, along with none other than Paul Revere, who was in charge of the artillery. Revere was exonerated but Saltonstall, tagged with the full responsibility, was condemned never to hold another command. The two American generals present, Solomon Lovell and Peleg Wadsworth (the grandfather of the poet Henry Wadsworth Longfellow), were actually praised for their efforts to contain the fiasco that resulted in the total destruction of the Yankee fleet. Saltonstall's fault was that he continually refused to attack, even though the American forces, upon arrival at the mouth of the Penobscot, significantly outnumbered the British. For more than two weeks, Saltonstall dithered. Then, a powerful armada of British warships and transports bearing reinforcements appeared. The Americans tried to escape upriver and into Penobscot Bay and, thus scattered, were picked off by their pursuers, leaving a trail of wrecked and burning shipping all the way to Bangor.

The British grip on Castine and its surroundings now tightened. The effect was felt well down the coast, even as far south as Belfast and the Rockland area. Continual raiding made life on the offshore islands untenable. Even doughty soldiers like General Wadsworth were not secure. A raid by British commandos kidnapped him from his home in Thomaston. Wounded and incarcerated in Castine, Wadsworth showed his own mettle by soon escaping from his cell and fleeing in a canoe back across the American lines.

❧ NEW IRELAND: AN INTRIGUING MIGHT-HAVE-BEEN

Castine had become a Tory haven, protected by British bayonets. The next logical step was to turn it into a political entity. In the plans for a new province ruled the way the Loyalists wanted to see America ruled, there is a fascinating glimpse of how things might have stood had the Americans lost the Revolutionary War. The extent of New Ireland, as the putative province was to be called, consisted of almost all of Maine, from the Saco River east to the St. Croix. The governing authorities were to be a governor with a council, a chief justice and various civil officers, all paid by Parliament so that none would be dependent for their salaries on a provincial legislature, an extremely sore political point prior

3.14 General Knox's house, Montpelier, near Thomaston, was built in 1793 and suggests the grandeur of his ambition as a major landowner in the District of Maine. A modern reproduction of the house now stands on the site.

The BOXER and ENTERPRIZE.

3.15

3.16

to the Revolution. In fact, there was to be no colonial legislature until the King decided conditions were suitable. The council or upper house would be appointed for life and would constitute an American House of Lords.

Landholding would be confined to loyal Tories. All others would have to be tenants and pay rents for their land. The Church of England would be the established religion. Huge estates would be granted in order to "lay the ground of an Aristocratic Power." Democracy, American style, was not to be the style of New Ireland.

But not all Tories supported this scheme. One of the most notorious and powerful, the former Governor of Massachusetts Thomas Hutchinson, called it "preposterous" and vigorously intrigued behind the scenes to kill the idea, which was the brainchild of Dr. John Calef (pronounced "calf"), an Ipswich, Massachusetts, ex-member of the General Court. Hutchinson's motive was to prevent Massachusetts from being dismembered. His belief in an ultimate British victory predisposed him to

∿

3.15 *(facing page)* H.M.S. BOXER *vs.* U.S.S. ENTERPRISE, *painted about 20 years after the 1813 naval battle. This American victory 40 miles off Portland Harbor, in which both captains were mortally wounded, was one of the most dramatic events in Maine during the War of 1812.*

∿

3.16 *View of Paris Hill (1802), an overmantel by an unknown artist from the Lazarus Hathaway House in Paris, depicts a central theme of Maine in the early 19th century: the clearing of the forests and the advance of civilization.*

3.17

3.17 *Pownalborough Court House (1761), on the eastern bank of the Kennebec, was the scene of much bitter litigation in the two decades before statehood between absentee landlords and their agents, on the one hand, and the settlers who had cleared and occupied what they considered unclaimed land, on the other.*

believe that he would one day be back at the helm of his native province, and he wanted it left intact.

The King's Attorney General, Alexander Wedderburn, also contributed to the plan's demise. He argued that the authorized borders of pre-Revolutionary Massachusetts, which included Maine, remained unimpaired despite the rebellion and that the English government had no right to detach land from the ex-Bay Colony. Once the existing British military government was withdrawn when the redcoats evacuated Castine in 1783, the jurisdiction of Massachusetts automatically resumed.

Throughout the Revolution, Maine soldiers and sailors could be found everywhere, not only at home defending their hearths. The major battles were fought beyond Maine's borders and there were Mainers in some of the most famous of them, like Yorktown, Saratoga, and Bunker Hill, and at Valley Forge. John Paul Jones's first ship, the RANGER, was built in Maine, and a York man, Thomas Simpson, eventually took over its command. Another York man, Lieutenant Moses Banks, served on George Washington's staff. And after the war, many veterans emigrated to Maine, receiving land as a reward for their services. The most renowned of them, General Henry Knox, Washington's first Secretary of War, received his land in a different fashion. He married the granddaughter of Samuel Waldo and fell heir to the vast Waldo holdings. It was a situation that was in part responsible for the next great crisis to shake the populace. Maine had helped win independence from England. Before long, they were struggling with the notion of breaking away from Massachusetts.

3.18

3.18 *John G. Brown's* Bowdoin Campus, *c. 1822. Chartered in 1794 in an effort to "civilize the wilderness," Bowdoin College became embroiled in the religious and political controversies of the two decades that preceded statehood. Identified with the Congregationalists, Bowdoin soon found it had a Baptist rival in Waterville, now known as Colby College (chartered in 1813). Free Will Baptists founded Bates College in Lewiston in 1855, and the University of Maine followed at Orono in 1865.*

4.1

MAINE AND STATEHOOD

∾ THE STRUGGLE FOR SEPARATION

AN ACROSTIC IN MAINE'S FIRST NEWSPAPER, the *Falmouth Gazette*, in 1785 signalled the start of a movement that would take 35 years to reach fruition. Signed by "a benevolent Gentleman in a neighboring Town," the mysterious notice, when deciphered, alluded to the putative city as the soon-to-be capital of "a rising state." Other anonymous contributions from "A Farmer," "Ruricola," and "Impartalis" added to the support for breakaway action. By the fall, a meeting to discuss the issue was announced. Among the 30 men who attended were some weighty individuals, including General Peleg Wadsworth and his eventual son-in-law Stephen Longfellow. A seven-member committee drew up plans for a larger gathering on January 4, 1786.

Massachusetts responded with hostility. In Boston, Governor James Bowdoin—a major absentee landowner in the District of Maine—railed against the separatists. Charges flew that they were involved in an insurrection against the Commonwealth and that statehood for Maine would open the door for Tory refugees to return from Canada. The Maine patriots refuted these claims and submitted a list of grievances, reasons why they should separate, such as the location of the State Supreme Court in distant Boston, trade regulations reducing the price of lumber, and excessive taxes.

Before the next meeting of the dissidents, Shays's Rebellion broke out in western Massachusetts. A disagreement over tactics then split the Maine forces; the more conservative wanted to hold off demanding separation until after the furor over the outbreak had died down; a radical faction, led by General Samuel Thompson, the Brunswick militia commander who had brought Mowatt's wrath upon Falmouth, insisted they confront Boston at once. When Thompson failed to go to Boston immediately to present his demands and subsequently seemed to become more interested in opposing ratification of the U.S. Constitution, the independence agitation in Maine sputtered to a halt.

∾

4.1 *Charles Codman*, State House, Augusta, *1836. Built of Hallowell granite in 1829-32, the capitol was intended by its designer, Charles Bulfinch, to resemble his Massachusetts State House in Boston.*

4.2

~

4.2 *Gilbert Stuart,* Governor William

King, 1806. *King was the prime mover in*

the effort to separate Maine from

Massachusetts and in 1820 became the new

state's first governor.

But the idea refused to die. Resuscitated in the 1790s, it met its initial elective test in May 1792—and failed! The voters of Maine rejected statehood for themselves by a margin of 2,524 to 2,074.

Another vote five years later in May 1797 reversed this thin plurality of negative votes and approved statehood, 2,785 to 2,412. But the Massachusetts General Court deemed that a mandate of 373 was insufficient; also, it pointed out that scarcely more than 5,000 citizens out of a population of 100,000 had bothered to go to the polls.

The next vote was not to be for another ten years.

It was a disaster for the separatists. Statehood was rejected by an almost three to one landslide, 9,404 to 3,370.

As often happens in politics, however, out of the ashes of defeat there rises phoenix-like the elements of a future victory. A real change in Maine was the make-up of the leadership of those who were seeking statehood. It had become a party issue. It was the Democrat-Republican Party of Thomas Jefferson that was now leading the fight for separation. At the head of the Jeffersonians was a wealthy shipowner and merchant from Bath named William King. He had once belonged to the opposing Federalist Party but had converted and in 1805 was elected to the General Court. That same year, the Democrat-Republicans carried Maine for the first time for their Maine-born gubernatorial candidate James Sullivan.

The crushing defeat for statehood in 1807 was attributed to the fact that the economic times were simply too good; people didn't want a change. Then came the "Embargo of 1807," Jefferson's ill-considered plan to keep the U.S. neutral in the Anglo-French rivalry of the Napoleonic Wars, and, following that disaster, the War of 1812.

Although the Democrat-Republicans suffered politically from the economic losses caused by the Embargo, their Federalist rivals hurt themselves even more by opposing the war and even hinting at their famous Hartford Convention in 1815 that New England might secede from the country. Particularly damaging to Massachusetts's continued control of Maine was the Bay State's failure to protect its easternmost district from the British, who had invaded and held almost all of eastern Maine for the duration of the war.

INDEPENDENCE ! !
July 26th, 1819.

CITIZENS OF MAINE,

Shall Maine be a free, sovereign and independent State, or shall you and your children remain forever the servants of a foreign power ? This is the true question that is to be settled by your votes on *Monday next.* The friends of liberty cannot hesitate in the choice between freedom and servitude.

What shall we lose by separation ? the privilege of being governed by Massachusetts. What shall we gain ? the right of governing ourselves.

☞ The last year we paid Massachusetts EIGHTY EIGHT THOUSAND DOLLARS for governing us. This is proved by the OFFICIAL CERTIFICATE signed by the SECRETARY OF STATE. It will cost us less, probably not more than ONE HALF this sum to govern ourselves. Almost the whole of this is now carried to Boston and expended there. Choose *freedom and independence* and *one half of this sum* will be saved to the people, and the *other half will be spent* at home.

☞ *Six Millions of acres* of Lands in Maine are now owned by *non-resident land holders ;* full *one third* of which is *owned in England.* These lands now pay but a *nominal tax.* Two THIRDS of the tax is taken off ; and who pays it ? ☞ It is paid by the FARMER AND MECHANIC *in addition* to his own proper share of taxes. ☜ It is these non-resident land holders who are afraid of taxes. ☞ Their land is taxed at *two per cent,* yours at *six per cent.*

☞ They now pay a *Boston lawyer* ONE OR TWO THOUSAND DOLLARS A YEAR to manage this business with the legislature. *What is taken from their tax is added to yours.* Their taxes may be increased but yours will be diminished.

These land holders are now traversing Maine in every direction. They have their *agents in pay* in every quarter, and they are all *opposed to your independence.*

If you do not wish that you and your children should forever *pay the taxes of these nabobs of Massachusetts and ENGLAND,* turn out on the next Monday and give your voices for separation.

FELLOW CITIZENS,

The eyes of all America are upon you. Your enemies are active and vigilant, and already boast of their fancied success. We exhort you to turn out in your whole strength. Let not a vote be lost. Leave your private business for a day or half a day or an hour, and convince the world by an overwhelming majority that you deserve FREEDOM AND INDEPENDENCE.

July 21.

4.3

∾

4.3 *Independence broadside, 1819, urging*

separation of the District of Maine from Massachusetts.

Statehood became a reality the next year.

4.4

4.5

4.5 The Rev. Jonathan Fisher's A Morning View of Blue Hill Village of 1824 is perhaps the most famous icon of Maine in the Early Republic. The background is an accurate topographical depiction of Blue Hill; the foreground presents allegorical figures expressing various virtues and vices.

William King had been a major general of the Massachusetts militia in charge of protecting Maine. But he had not been able to procure the slightest help from the Boston establishment to finance an offensive to drive the British back into Canada. Even a personal visit to the governor had been of no avail.

King had other complaints, as well, against Massachusetts. One of them involved religion and two educational institutions in Maine—Bowdoin College, identified with the Congregational Church, long dominant in Massachusetts and the recipient of public funds from the General Court, and Waterville College (later Colby), a new Baptist institution, struggling to establish itself. A trustee of Bowdoin, King quarrelled with the college over a financial matter and threw his support to the Baptists. As a Representative in the General Court, he had repeatedly sought, in vain, to secure some public funds for the Waterville college. The issue, in his mind, had become one of sectarian tolerance versus religious monopoly. Politically, it was not a coincidence that there had been a dramatic increase of Baptist congregations in Maine. By 1820, they outnumbered the Congregationalists.

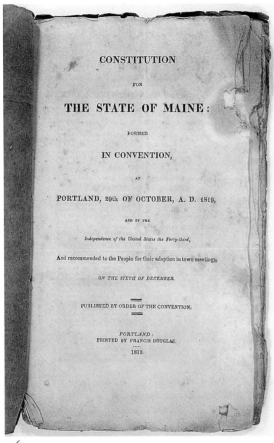

4.6a

∾

4.6a *and* 4.6b

The Maine State Constitution.

Another political development in Maine was the growing strength of the "squatter" population. Great landowners like Henry Knox became villains in the eyes of many common people, especially those who had settled on lands they did not own but had improved and now regarded as their rightful property. The "White Indian" activity in the backcountry almost turned into a civil war, as squatters harassed the proprietors' surveyors, and landowners threatened severe retaliation. The Democrat-Republican Party became the champion of the settlers and William King their especial hero when he was able to secure passage of the Betterment Act of 1807, which required proprietors to pay for any improvements if they evicted people who had occupied land for more than six years.

Two new votes on statehood in 1816 again did not result in victory for the separatists, but their momentum was gaining. Moreover, the Democrat-Republican ascendancy in the District of Maine was causing Massachusetts Federalists to reconsider their opposition. Maybe it was time to jettison those mavericks who cut so deeply into the Federalist vote. Then, in March 1819, William King was able, with the aid of his half-brother Rufus, a U.S. Senator from New York, to have the "Coasting Law" repealed by Congress.

This measure, which had been on the books since the creation of the United States, had been a severe impediment to statehood for Maine. It would have meant that shipowners in Maine, sending their vessels beyond New Hampshire, had to stop in every state and pay a tax, since the law required such payments in every noncontiguous state. With Maine a part of Massachusetts, Rhode Island and Connecticut and New York were also contiguous, but Maine alone had only New Hampshire as a buffer.

This psychological breakthrough brought new support to statehood from the coastal towns of Maine. The next vote, 17,091 to 7,132, was a landslide for the separatists.

Nevertheless, as in a thriller with a suspenseful ending, the perils were not over. There was a deadline that had to be met, March 4, 1820, imposed by the conditions of the Massachusetts bill allowing Maine to break away. If Congress had not ratified Maine as a new state by that date, then all bets were off.

Again with the assistance of his half-brother Rufus, William King began lobbying in Washington. Yet a seemingly insurmountable barrier faced them—the refusal of the South to admit another free state into the Union without a corresponding slave state to "balance" it. For Rufus King, leader of the antislavery forces in Congress, this was a particularly delicate question. Nor was it easy for Maine's own Representatives in the Massachusetts Congressional delegation to overcome their antislavery principles and adopt the "Missouri Compromise." But adopt it they finally did, as did the Congress.

On March 15, 1820, Maine officially became the 23rd state of the Union.

∞ ORGANIZING THE STATE

The bill passed by the Massachusetts General Court that allowed Maine to secede not only set a deadline but also required the Mainers to hold a constitutional convention prior to statehood. Thus, on October 12, 1819, 274 delegates representing nearly all of Maine's incorporated towns filed into the First Parish Church in Portland. Under the guidance of William King, who was promptly chosen to preside, they hammered out a document that was sent to the voters on December 6, 1819, and received almost unanimous approval.

Yet the deliberations in the First Parish Church had been full of contentions. What the state should be named was one. "Maine" was obviously the favored suggestion, but an Augusta delegate, Daniel Cony, moved to substitute "Columbus." His odd logic was that the U.S. Navy had begun naming battleships for states and that they would have to wait a long time for the Maine to join the list; however, there already was a dreadnought called the COLUMBUS, so the honor was ready-made. Little could Daniel Cony ever imagine the ultimate fate of a battleship MAINE as he went down to defeat in his quest.

Even the use of the term "state" was contested. Many of the delegates preferred to continue the use of "commonwealth," which was (and still is) the official designation for Massachusetts. Others argued that the "Commonwealth of Maine" sounded too highfalutin. Still, the outcome was close. The "State o' Maine" became a "state" by only six votes.

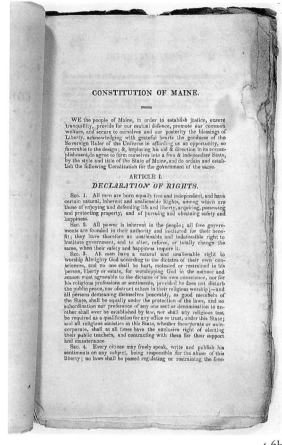

4.6b

4.7

~

4.7 *Maine's first official State Militia Color, printed on white silk by John Penniman of Boston in 1822.*

4.8 *Lemuel Moody's* Signals at Portland Lighthouse *(1807) offers four views of the busy harbor as well as the local merchants' signal flags, on the eve of an event—Jefferson's Embargo—that was to cripple maritime trade throughout New England.*

4.8

4.9

∾

4.9 *One of the earliest depictions of Mount*

Katahdin is among the watercolors reproduced as

colored plates in Charles T. Jackson's First

Report on the Geology of the State of

Maine *(Augusta, 1837). Jackson sought not only*

to correct earlier maps and present scientific data

but also to encourage proper development of the

state's mineral and water resources.

4.10 A note from Congressman Mark Hill in Washington to future Governor William King informing him of the passage of the famous compromise in 1820 which resulted in one new free state (Maine) and one new slave state (Missouri).

The size of the Legislature was also fiercely debated. The small, rural communities wanted the Massachusetts model of one representative for every 150 electors. An unwieldy body of 700 to 1,000 members would have been the result, given Maine's more liberal franchise. Cities like Portland, meanwhile, were pushing for the smallest number of legislators possible. The veteran politician John Holmes of Alfred headed a committee that offered a compromise of 151 House members, the number it remains today, although not without constant challenge. The State Senate, Holmes' group recommended, should also depart from Massachusetts practice. There, the wealth of the county determined its number of Senate members; in Maine, it was to be population. The maximum number of Senators was set at 31 and since has been raised to 35, but State Senators are no longer elected entirely within county lines due to the "one person, one vote" principle.

Still more deviations from the "mother state" followed. There were to be no property qualifications for voting. In Massachusetts, you had to have an income of at least $10 or an estate worth $200. Nor did the Mainers want a Lieutenant Governor. The President of the Senate would succeed to the top office if the Governor died or couldn't continue. Hotly debated was another Massachusetts constitutional provision that people had "a duty to worship." The Maine delegates insisted on absolute freedom of religion, as well as freedom from religious observation, even when nonsectarian.

William King, despite some antipapist grumblings against toleration for Catholics, saw his fight with Bowdoin College dealt with in Article VIII's provision that the state could grant no funds to a "literary institution" (i.e., Bowdoin) unless the state had the power to overturn decisions of the trustees. Article VIII, by the way, which was entitled "Education," had been drafted in large part at William King's request by his political ally Thomas Jefferson.

Armed with an accepted constitution, Maine was ready to assume the responsibilities of statehood as soon as the word came from Washington.

On March 16, 1820, a day after Congress' action, cannon salutes were fired all day in Portland, and a magnificent ball was held that evening with William King as guest of honor.

The gubernatorial election was scheduled for April, but the choice of King for the post was a foregone conclusion. He began working at the job even before the vote, since he was the only candidate. The elected Legislature assembled at Portland in late May and received its first message from the chief executive on June 2. The chambers were situated on the site of an old stable and swarms of flies were a constant plague on warm days.

The session ran until June 28 and the lawmakers passed 32 acts and 36 resolves. As requested by the Governor in his opening address, a State Supreme Court was created. Two U.S. Senators were elected, John Holmes and General John Chandler, chosen as U.S Senators then were, by the dominant party in the Legislature, the Democrat-Republicans. While the Jeffersonians controlled most state offices, King lived up to his promise to give the opposing Federalists one third of the spoils. In fact, the Chief Justice he named for the Supreme Court was a Federalist, Prentiss Mellen.

A State Seal was devised, bearing a pine tree, a "Moose Deer," a farmer, a sailor, the North Star (as Maine was then the northernmost state), and the motto, *Dirigo*, Latin for "I lead." Placed against a field of dark blue, it embellished the new State Flag.

The Legislature, having heard the Governor give a financial report—total revenues were $60,486—set up a salary schedule for the administration and themselves and authorized paying the state's bills. The largest was $500 for printing. The artisan who had manufactured the State Seal received $50. There was a complaint that the metallic stamp he made had not been "ingeniously wrought." But, in any case, Maine was officially in business.

4.10

4.11

4.12

4.12 *Charles H. Granger's* Muster Day, Saco, *depicts a familiar scene in Maine towns of the 1840s—the local militia gathering for an exercise that was often more social and political than military. The militia drills attracted carnivalesque crowds, including peddlers, gamblers, and itinerant preachers.*

❧

4.11 *(facing page) The economic prosperity of early 19th-century Maine is reflected in the decorative and practical arts of the time. Fourteen-year-old Caroline McKenney's sampler, c. 1823, showing Old Second Parish Church and her father's hostelry in Portland. A flintlock pistol, c. 1811-17, made by John Hall of Portland. A detail of Hall's famous flintlock sporting rifle, 1811, showing its curly maple stock and tiger stripe graining. A major technical breakthrough, the breechloading rifle was faster to load and more accurate to fire than standard military rifles of the day. Hall, rather than Eli Whitney, may have been the first to employ mass manufacture of interchangeable parts. His rifle was widely used in the Indian wars and the Mexican War. A pink luster pitcher, possibly Staffordshire, celebrating American naval victories in the War of 1812.*

❧ THE STATE CAPITAL CONTROVERSY

It wasn't the flies that stirred those early Maine lawmakers into seeking to remove the capital from Portland. It had been understood from the beginning that southern Maine was too remote from what was expected to be the center of the state. Just as Philadelphia and New York City served as U.S. capitals before Washington, D.C., Portland knew it would be displaced. That the process took twelve years was not anticipated and could be chalked up to the Forest City's resistance. Indeed, not until after Portland made a nearly successful effort in 1907 to move the capital back from Augusta was the matter put to rest. An amendment to the State Constitution finally enshrined Augusta as Maine's political place of business.

As far back as 1821, the Legislature formed a committee to search for a new site. Its first choice was Hallowell, then a thriving port on the Kennebec. But Hallowell had an insuperable disadvantage. The lawmakers were overwhelmingly Democrat-Republicans. The wealthy landowners on the Kennebec mostly voted Federalist.

So it was back to the drawing board with another committee, this time stacked by the Jeffersonians. They eventually chose an area also on the Kennebec, a stone's throw from Hallowell, but in another community. Actually, Augusta was a mere village where they were offered free land by Judge Nathaniel Weston, Weston's Hill, overlooking the river. The legislators in Portland confirmed the committee's choice and designated the first Wednesday of January 1827 as the date when the Legislature had to meet in its new home.

Portland's representatives managed to stall the process for five more years. Eventually, they were outmaneuvered, the well-known architect Charles Bulfinch was hired, and ex-Governor William King was made clerk-of-the-works to superintend the construction.

Despite his vigilence, cost overruns plagued the project. Instead of the initial $60,000 appropriation, the ultimate expenditure reached $140,000. The cornerstone was laid on July 4, 1829 and, in a patriotic mood, Major Augustus Davezac, the personal emissary of President Andrew Jackson, alluded to the storm that was gathering over Maine's still undefined northern border with British-controlled Canada. "The frontiers of Maine will never recede before the footsteps of an invader," he declared.

The state government, both executive and legislative, eventually housed in Bulfinch's handsome, granite-faced edifice in 1832, had almost a decade of uncertainty as to whether Davezac's prediction would come true.

4.13

4.13 *An early 19th-century mourning picture for Sarah Wentworth of Buxton, made by her sister Eunice, who succeeded her as the wife of the clockmaker Robert Wentworth.*

5.1

MAINE COMES OF AGE

❧ THE SITUATION IN AROOSTOOK

WHEN THE PLENIPOTENTIARIES OF GREAT BRITAIN and the soon-to-be United States of America sat down in a town house in Paris in 1783 to work out a peace agreement, they were not particularly meticulous about every detail. To determine the boundaries between the new country and Canada, the language became downright fuzzy. In the case of Maine, on the east and the north a line was to be drawn from the "source of the St. Croix River" until it reached the "highlands dividing the rivers that empty themselves in the River St. Lawrence from those which fall into the Atlantic Ocean," at which point it would be terminated.

Fifteen years were to pass before Jay's Treaty fixed the true source of the St. Croix River. That took care of the eastern boundaries. But still, after endless discussions, neither side could agree where the "highlands" were.

The British argued that they were at Mars Hill, which would have given them a good chunk of what is today Maine's Aroostook County.

The Americans staked their claim on the Notre Dame Mountains. This would have extended Maine to within 20 miles of the St. Lawrence River.

The Madawaska region, lying at the heart of the contested area, had been inhabited since the end of the American Revolution by French-speaking Acadians. They had originally been driven from their Nova Scotia homes during the 1750s and then once again displaced from the lower St. John River when Tory exiles had taken over their property. For years, no one had bothered them on the upper St. John, and their numbers had been increased by other French speakers from Quebec and a smattering of Irish Catholics.

❧

5.1 *Fitz Hugh Lane*, Castine Harbor, 1852.

The Luminist painter was among the first major

American artists to explore the distinctive effects of

light and water along the coast of Maine.

5.2

~

5.2 *A 19th-century drawing of the block-house at Fort Kent, an important American stronghold in the St. John Valley at a time when quarrels over lumbering on the disputed border with British Canada threatened war.*

In 1817, the first Americans appeared on the Madawaska scene. The most famous of the new arrivals was John Baker, who settled north of Fort Kent and founded a community called Baker's Brook—an American community, flying Old Glory and celebrating the Fourth of July. Unilaterally, Baker declared that the entire region belonged to Maine and petitioned the Maine Legislature to grant him legal ownership.

The authorities in New Brunswick were not pleased. After an incident in which a Canadian envoy removed an American flag and saw it promptly replaced, a sheriff was sent from Fredericton, and Baker was arrested and imprisoned.

The affair assumed international significance. The U.S. Secretary of State and the Governor of Maine vigorously protested. Maine militiamen marched to Houlton and began building a military road, leading toward Canada. Then, arbitration was agreed to, and King William of Holland was chosen to render an impartial decision as to whose land it was. His judgment on how to split the difference between the rival claims was swiftly rejected by both sides.

The Maine Legislature passed a law incorporating the Madawaska region, known to be a rich source of timber. Rather than acquiesce, Governor Sir Archibald Campbell of New Brunswick sent his troops to the scene. John Baker, having been freed, feared reincarceration and fled to Portland. He later convinced President Andrew Jackson to speak out on the matter.

The lull that followed after tempers cooled lasted for seven years. The issue lay dormant yet hardly forgotten.

∾ GOVERNOR FAIRFIELD AND "THE AROOSTOOK WAR"

In January 1839, John Fairfield of Saco became Governor of Maine. Previously, he had served Maine in the U.S. House of Representatives. His maiden speech there had been on the northeast boundary question, a two-hour oration that was well received. Its stern tone was best expressed in his statement that "in Maine, there is but one feeling on this subject, that State, sir, feels that she has suffered deep and enduring wrong at the hands of the British government."

Meanwhile, an incident occurred, totally unrelated to the boundary dispute, that propelled this obscure Congressman from Maine into the national limelight. The event was the death of his fellow Maine Congressman Jonathan Cilley in a duel with Kentucky Representative William Graves. The notoriety in this case was not that a Congressman (Cilley) had been killed but that a Congressman (Fairfield) had spoken out against the practice of dueling, thereby breaking an unwritten rule in Congress not to mention the practice. The publicity Fairfield generated helped him win the governorship.

Where the northeast boundary was concerned, the new Maine chief executive soon showed what a "hawk" he was on the question. He dispatched a land agent accompanied by a sheriff's posse to Aroostook to drive off New Brunswick loggers who were harvesting timber—an act Fairfield declared illegal and one that he said had deprived the state of $100,000 worth of wood.

5.3

∾

5.3 *The distinctive vernacular architecture of Acadian houses in the St. John Valley of far northern Maine serves as a visual link with the French-speaking settlements of New Brunswick.*

5.4 A Micmac Indian, depicted in the early 19th-century by Lt. Robert Petley. Much of Maine's Native American population was destroyed by disease or warfare in the 18th-century; many of their survivors in the 19th-century lived economically marginal lives, based on trapping, hunting, fishing, and working as guides.

〜

5.5 (facing page) Victor de Grailly, Eastport and Passamaquoddy Bay, c. 1840. While a highly romanticized view of a fishing village—the painter depicts the citizenry wearing the Parisian fashions of the day—this landscape suggests the allure the Maine coast was beginning to hold for distant artists.

5.4

Unfortunately, the Mainers were literally caught napping, arrested in their sleep by a larger group of armed Canadians.

With his people in jail in Fredericton, Fairfield ordered his militia to the north country. He also called up more than 10,000 officers and men as reserves and won an appropriation from the Legislature of $800,000 for "a sufficient military force...to prevent further depredations on the public lands and to protect the timber..."

The British, in turn, marched 800 Irish fusiliers west from New Brunswick and 500 red-coated regulars east from Quebec. At Cabano, the King's soldiers built Fort Ingall. To the south of them, the Mainers built Fort Kent and Fort Fairfield. Both sides were poised for war. Even the release of the American prisoners did not calm tensions.

In Washington, Congress empowered President Martin Van Buren to raise 50,000 volunteers and appropriate $10 million. A Maine Congressman, George Evans, took to the floor of the House to boast that whether or not they were given Federal help, Maine people would resist. In Augusta, Governor Fairfield reviewed his troops on horseback while thousands of spectators watched.

Oddly enough, it was a U.S. Army general who played the role of a peacemaker. Van Buren ordered General Winfield Scott to Maine with copies of a memorandum worked out between the State Department and the British Foreign Ministry, which called for a withdrawal of the Maine forces. Knowing the outrage this agreement would provoke, General Scott was able to convert its language, if not its essence, into an acceptable face-saving formula. Both sides renounced the use of force. The Maine militia pulled back. The "Aroostook War" was over.

5.5

5.6

Guns had not blazed on the northeast frontier. Yet obviously the problem of the boundary had not been solved. Political battles within the United States, and to a lesser extent Maine, were to have their influence on the outcome. Maine voted ahead of the rest of the country in the national election of 1840, going to the polls in September rather than November. That year, the Whigs won in the Pine Tree State. General William Henry Harrison and his running mate, the ex-Democrat John Tyler, carried the normally Democratic state by 411 votes. Also winning election was the Whig candidate for Governor, Edward Kent. He had been Governor once before, had been beaten by John Fairfield and now, himself, beat Fairfield. In the closest election in Maine history, Fairfield really won the popular vote by nine votes, 45,588 to 45,579, but because 70 votes had been cast for other candidates, he had not gained an absolute majority. Under Maine law of the day, the election was thrown into the Legislature. Since that body was now dominated by the Whigs, Kent received the nod.

Ignoring these fine points of electoral history, the jubilant Whigs celebrated nationwide with a bit of campaign doggerel:

> *Oh, have you heard how Maine went?*
> *She went hell-bent for Governor Kent*
> *And Tippecanoe and Tyler, too.*
> *Tippecanoe and Tyler, too.*

5.7

5.8 *Surveying instruments from the early 19th-century serve as a reminder of how much of the interior of the state remained uninhabited, even uncharted, despite the establishment of townships on the maps.*

5.10 *(facing page) Total avoidance of alcohol—not merely temperance—was the message of this silk banner carried by the Dennysville Washingtonian Total Abstinence Society, painted in 1841 by John Regan of Eastport.*

5.9 *"Plan of the British and American Positions in the Disputed Territory By an Eye Witness," Nathaniel Dearborn's multi-colored lithograph printed by Bouve and Sharp in Boston in 1843, four years after the Aroostook "crisis." The disposition of troops may not be entirely accurate, but the mapmaker has conveyed the seriousness of the situation.*

5.9

5.8

As Maine went, in this case, so went the nation. "Tippecanoe" Harrison and Tyler gained the White House. New England's own Daniel Webster, who had once taught school in Fryeburg, Maine, became the U.S. Secretary of State.

Webster wanted to settle the northeast boundary question peaceably. His overtures to the British finally brought the welcome response that Lord Ashburton would be sent to negotiate.

Lord Ashburton had been born Alexander Baring. He, too, had ties to Maine. He was married to the daughter of Robert Bingham, a Philadelphian who at the end of the American Revolution had bought up more than 2 million acres of Maine land. Baring's banking family had subsequently purchased many of those acres in helping the Binghams with their finances. The town of Baring in Washington County commemorates this role of the English firm. Daniel Webster, incidentally, had once done legal work for the Barings. The stage was therefore set for an amicable settlement.

The willingness of Webster and Ashburton to compromise faced many challenges. Webster's eagerness to accept half a loaf derived in part from his knowledge that a map existed with lines drawn on it by Benjamin Franklin during the 1783 peace treaty negotiations locating the boundary far south of the present American claim. The pressure Lord Ashburton felt to settle came also in part from the stiflingly hot Washington summer weather that was keeping him from sleeping. He was in the end willing to give up 7,000 of the 12,000 square miles in contention.

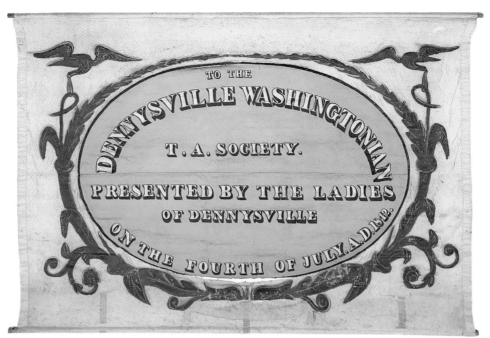

5.10a

5.10b

5.11 *Ambrotype of a young shoemaker, Bangor, c. 1860.*

5.12 *(facing page) A Maine cobbler's shop, c. 1850, as reconstructed for the "Made in Maine" exhibit at the Maine State Museum.*

5.11

Both men were severely criticized for their positions, once they had accepted terms. The Maine government, having reverted once again to the leadership of John Fairfield, made its displeasure loudly known. But Webster had a secret slush fund of $17,000, and he employed a wheeler-dealer Maine Congressman named F.O.J. ("Fog") Smith to spread the money around, particularly to newspaper editors. Once the Maine opposition faded, the U.S. Senate moved to ratify, and the vote was overwhelming, 39 to 9.

Eventually, Ashburton and Webster were lauded for their efforts, although the English authorities were miffed when the secret of the map Webster had suppressed at last became known. The line has remained ever since, unfortified and peaceably accepted.

5.13 *Firefighter John Hilling depicted the burning by a mob in 1854 of Bath's Old South Meeting House, which was being used as a Catholic church. The attack is evidence of the violence inspired in many towns by the "Know Nothing" Party's hostility toward Irish immigrants.*

✷

5.14 *(facing page) Congressman Jonathan Cilley, a college friend of Hawthorne, is best remembered for having been killed in a duel with a political foe.*

✷

5.15 *(facing page) Governor John Fairfield, commander of the Maine militia forces in the bloodless "Aroostook War" of 1839.*

5.13

❧ Rum, Romanism, Rebellion, and Republicans

Through the 1840s and 1850s, with roots even earlier, a trio of major political issues developed within the United States and were reflected in Maine public life. Later in the century, a Protestant clergyman in a sermon that had immense political repercussions, labelled them, in attention-grabbing alliteration: "Rum, Romanism and Rebellion."

Adding another "R," it can be said they contributed to the creation of the Republican Party, which was to dominate Maine politics after 1856.

Rebellion—and the related issue of slavery as perceived in the North—had already played its part in the birth of Maine as a state, through the Missouri Compromise. As inhabitants of the state the most distant from the South, it might have been expected that the Mainers could have stayed out of the controversy until it exploded nationwide. But so volatile was the issue that a simple incident, happening thousands of miles from Maine, could embroil the government of the Pine Tree State in a severe and long-lasting dispute with a fellow state below the Mason-Dixon Line. In 1837, a Maine schooner, the SUSAN, stopped at Savannah, Georgia, to undergo minor repairs. When she sailed away a few days later, the captain and crew were unaware that a slave laborer named Atticus, who had worked on her, had stowed aboard.

Once his disappearance was discovered, Atticus' owners surmised that he might have gone on the SUSAN. They set off in pursuit but never caught up until after the ship reached Maine and docked at Thomaston. Upon arrival, the Georgians immediately went to court and obtained a warrant of arrest for the fugitive slave. Eventually, Atticus was betrayed to them for a $20 reward. An angry demonstration on the dock at East Thomaston did not prevent them from leaving with their "recovered property."

The matter might have rested there had it not been for the slaveholders' lack of judgment. They applied in a Georgia court for the arrest of the SUSAN's captain and first mate on the grounds that they had deliberately abducted a slave and further demanded that Maine extradite the two to stand trial. Indignantly the Governor of Maine refused. The Georgia Legislature then toyed with the idea of arresting all Maine citizens who visited their state and holding them as hostages.

5.14

5.15

∾

5.16 *Hannibal Hamlin, one of the leaders of the new Republican Party in Maine in the late 1850s and vice president of the United States in Lincoln's first term (1861-65).*

∾

5.18 *(facing page) Harriet Beecher Stowe, while living in Brunswick in 1850-52, wrote* Uncle Tom's Cabin, *one of the most influential books of the 19th-century.*

Although no extreme actions ultimately were taken by Georgia, the affair continued to poison relations between the two states. Governor Edward Kent, when he assumed office, was also asked to deliver up the two men. He likewise refused, as did his successor John Fairfield, who had to respond to a threat from Georgia that any Maine person visiting within the Peach Tree State's borders would be assumed to do so with the express intent of stealing slaves from their owners.

Maine's first antislavery society was formed in 1833. But abolition in those early decades of the 19th century was viewed as a radical measure, not a respectable political position, especially in a state with extensive commercial ties with the South. The Democratic Party, for the most part, was still "soft" on slavery, preferring to avoid any discussion of it that might anger its Southern wing. At a party convention in Maine, it was openly declared that "resistance to the Fugitive Slave Law [of 1850] is as criminal as to any other law and he who encourages it encourages anarchy."

Yet, as sentiment against slavery began to intensify in the North after 1850, the internal split in the dominant party slowly surfaced. Personifying the change was a Democratic Congressman named Hannibal Hamlin. Still a Democrat, he defeated the proslavery Nathan Clifford in the election held by the Legislature in 1848 to choose a U.S. Senator. And in slightly more than a dozen years, he was the Republican Vice President of the United States, elected for Abraham Lincoln's first term.

By 1853, the antislavery Democrats in Maine were running their own candidates. In 1855, groups disenchanted with both the Democrats and the Whigs met in the small Franklin County town of Strong and formed the Maine branch of the national Republican Party that had been first organized in Michigan the year before. In 1856, Hamlin, running as a Republican, was overwhelmingly elected Governor.

Maine's effect on the raging national debate was not only political. In 1852, a book written in Maine by the wife of a Bowdoin College professor was published. Harriet Beecher Stowe had come to Brunswick two years earlier from Cincinatti with her husband Calvin, a theologian. According to Stowe family tradition, while in Brunswick's First Parish Church one morning in February 1851, Mrs. Stowe had a vision. She "saw" an elderly slave being beaten to death and forgiving his murderers. This flash of imagination turned into an important chapter of *Uncle Tom's Cabin*, which was not solely a sensational international best seller; it also became a political weapon of such devastating impact that when Abraham Lincoln finally met the professor's wife, he reportedly addressed her as "the little lady who started the big war."

Of the forces making up the newly formed Republican Party, only a part represented the Free Soilers, those who wanted to prevent the spread of unfree labor into the new states of the West. Another issue of raging importance that brought recruits flocking to the GOP was "temperance," the fight against Demon Rum.

ꙮ NEAL DOW AND THE MAINE LAW

Not widely known in the United States is the fact that Maine was the first state to pass a prohibition law. In fact, for many years after it was passed in 1851, such legislation was generically referred to by the term, "Maine Law." Forever identified with this significant political event, which helped solidify Republican strength by the party's appeal to all those who wished to ban the consumption of liquor, was the "Napoleon of Temperance," a Portlander named Neal Dow, who had been crusading since the 1820s to turn Maine dry.

At the time when Neal Dow, a member of the Deluge Engine Company of volunteer firemen in Portland, persuaded his fellows to give up serving liquor at their annual celebrations, drinking alcoholic beverages was probably even more pervasive than it is today. The "musters" of the local militia companies were noted for being little more than drunken bashes. The West Indies trade provided an ample supply of cheap rum, and it was not unusual to pay workers by the pint.

Neal Dow set out to change all this, becoming a founding member of the Maine Temperance Society in 1827 but then splitting with it when some members insisted they should be allowed to continue to imbibe wine, "a gentleman's drink." Forming his own Maine Temperance Union, Dow teamed up with an ex-War of 1812 general, James Appleton, now a state legislator, to introduce a prohibition measure in Augusta. It failed of passage, but the first shot had been fired.

5.18

ꙮ

5.17 *Henry Wadsworth Longfellow, the most widely read American poet of the 19th-century, recalled his childhood and young adulthood in Maine in such works as* My Lost Youth *and* Morituri Salutamus.

5.17

5.19

5.19 *Domestic wares c. 1820-50 showed an increasing emphasis on comfort and a willingness to adapt high styles to middle-class pocketbooks. Good examples are furnished by interior Maine's distinctive painted furniture, as in this chair, bed, and chest. Forms were basic, but surfaces were ornamented with elaborate graining or floral motives, typically painted yellow, green, or red. The quilt, oil lamps, and glazed stoneware are other characteristic household goods of the time. The mural is a detail from Rufus Porter's work in the 1830s in the Benjamin House in Winthrop.*

5.20

5.21

5.20 *(facing page)* "The Log Cabin and Hard Cider Political Club," a Portland group of Whigs photographed in the 1850s, a time when the Whig Party was about to be absorbed into the new Republican Party. This is one of the earliest group portrait daguerreotypes made in Maine to have survived.

5.21 Neal Dow, in later years in the library of his Portland home. Mayor of Portland and Civil War general, Dow was internationally known for his campaign against drinking alcohol, which in 1850 had resulted in the much-imitated Maine Law, a forerunner of national Prohibition.

Fourteen years later, Dow had his Maine Law. He then went barnstorming around the country, trying to persuade other states to follow his lead, which several did. In 1855, with the support of the newly formed Republican Party, Neal Dow was elected Mayor of Portland. Always outspoken and controversial, Dow squeaked into office by a mere 47 vote margin out of almost 4,000 votes cast, despite being attacked by one opposition newspaper as a "pimp, spy, fanatic, arrogant at heart."

His "arrogance" was almost his undoing in a monumental error of judgment he made over an affair that really was a technical triviality. It concerned liquor that a municipality could legally buy under the Maine Law for "medicinal and mechanical purposes." Portland's purchase of $1,600 worth

5.22

5.23

5.22 *(facing page) James Emery, View of Bucksport, c. 1850. Emery was a jeweler in Bucksport, on the Penobscot River, and also a talented amateur painter.*

5.23 *View of Portland Harbor and Forts, c. 1860. In the center is the granite Fort Gorges (1858), named to honor the 17th-century proprietor who never saw his vast Province of Maine. Although there was to be one daring Confederate raid into the harbor, the fort was never called upon fire its guns in anger.*

5.24 *J. B. Brown's* Portland Sugar Company, Portland, *c. 1855. In the decade before the Civil War, Portland began to emerge as a manufacturing center as well as a commercial entrepot. Brown's firm had prefected a method of converting molasses into sugar by using steam.*

5.24

of "medicinal" booze had been made under Dow's name as Mayor, not that of the city's purchasing agent. The opposition press, upon learning of this, claimed Dow would be making an illegal sale if he transferred it to an agent. With the issue thus whipped up, a crowd gathered at the store where the liquor was kept. Dow sent armed policemen to contain the throng, and when troublemakers began throwing rocks, the Mayor himself appeared at the head of a squad of rifle-toting militiamen. Despite the resistance of the captain in charge, Dow told the soldiers to open fire on the mob. Eventually, they did. One man was killed and seven wounded.

His political career shattered, Dow was actually put on trial for illegal liquor selling. Acquitted, he backed various gubernatorial candidates, with mixed results, and seemed on his way to a comeback when a temperance ally of his, a Congregational minister serving as Maine State Treasurer, was caught lending state money to private individuals, including Dow.

During the Civil War, Dow used his political connections in the Republican Party to become a regimental colonel and then a brigadier general. He was captured by the Confederates and later exchanged for a nephew of Robert E. Lee.

Tireless in his efforts against drinking, Dow ultimately ran for President on the Prohibition ticket and faded into oblivion as an irrelevant, even comical political figure. But the heritage of the issue he left behind him in Maine was to cement the GOP's strength in the state for decades to come.

Of the three "R"'s, Romanism was identified with the Irish Catholics, who had begun arriving in the state in considerable numbers after the potato famine of the late 1840s in Ireland. By the early 1850s, Bangor was one quarter Irish Catholic. Portland, by then, also included a large Gaelic enclave.

A few Irish Catholics already had been in Maine since the start of the 19th century. One of these pioneers was James Kavanagh, who settled in the Newcastle-Damariscotta area and helped erect St. Patrick's, the first English-speaking Catholic church in Maine.

Newcastle was then part of Massachusetts, whose laws were less tolerant than an independent Maine's were to be. James Kavanagh failed in an effort to relieve his coreligionists from having to pay support for the local Congregationalist minister. The French-born priest (later bishop) Jean Cheverus almost went to jail for performing a Catholic wedding in St. Patrick's. Indeed, it was James Kavanagh's son, Edward, who persuaded the framers of Maine's constitution to include complete religious toleration in their document and who afterward went on to a distinguished political career as a U.S. Congressman (the first Catholic from New England) and President of the Maine Senate and Governor of Maine (also the first Catholic chief executive in New England).

∾

5.25 *Nathaniel Hawthorne spent part of his childhood in Raymond then attended Bowdoin College (1821-25), which he fictionalized in his first novel,* Fanshawe.

5.25

5.26

5.27

But a particularly ugly manifestation of anti-Catholicism that became politicized in the so-called Native American, or "Know Nothing" Party, while more inflammatory in other parts of the country, also managed to tar Maine with its hate-filled brush. The most shameful hate crime during this period in Maine occurred in Ellsworth in October 1854. A gentle, courageous, Swiss-born priest, Father John Bapst, was on his way to Cherryfield to visit a sick parishioner and had decided to stay overnight in Ellsworth and say Mass the next morning. But a mob of local bully-boys broke into the house where he was staying, stripped him, tarred and feathered him, and rode him out of town on a rail. The imperturbable priest returned and held his Mass as planned.

A private high school in Bangor today commemorates Father Bapst's memory. But for a short time in 1855, the city— despite or perhaps because of its large Irish minority—had to suffer through a "Know Nothing" government. The dominant figure in this antiforeigner, antialcohol, lawandorder coalition was the Reverend Phillip Weaver, who was made city marshall, constable, superintendent of schools, and tax collector. The reign of Weaver, a friend of Neal Dow's, lasted but a short time, ending when it was discovered that he and his men had been selling the liquor they had confiscated and pocketing the proceeds and that Weaver, himself, was a heavy drinker.

5.26 (facing page) Charles E. Beckett's Winter Scene Near Portland of Dr. Cummings Driving His Fast Horse Jane Medora Which at One Time Carried the Mail to Canada depicts another stage in the Romantics' discovery of the Maine landscape: the beauty of winter. The neat, snug farmhouse also expresses mid-Victorian appreciation for domestic order and stability.

5.27 A mid 19th-century panorama of Belfast, on the Passagassawakeag River. Settled in 1770, the town became a prosperous port and seat of Waldo County, reaching a peak of population in 1860 of 5,520.

5.28 *A coin silver water pitcher presented to Mayor Neal Dow of Portland in recognition of his efforts on behalf of temperance.*

5.28

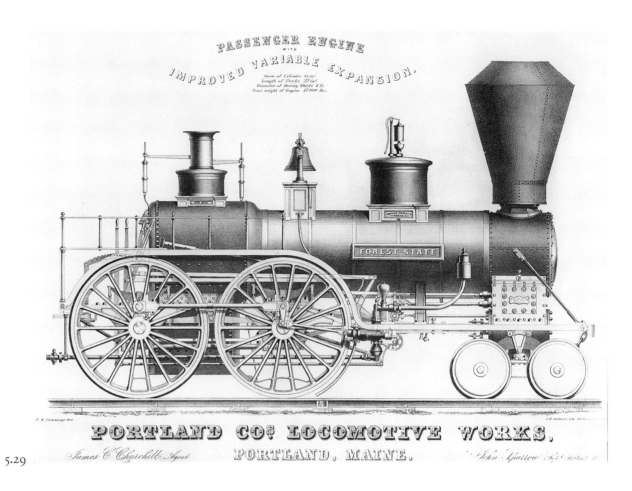

PASSENGER ENGINE
WITH
IMPROVED VARIABLE EXPANSION.

Diam. of Cylinder 15 in?
Length of Stroke 22 in?
Diameter of Driving Wheels 6 ft.
Total weight of Engine 57,000 lbs.

FOREST-STATE

PORTLAND C⁰⁵ LOCOMOTIVE WORKS,
PORTLAND, MAINE.

James C. Churchill Agent

5.29

In 1855, "Know-Nothing" support helped elect Anson P. Morrill, later a prominent Republican, as Governor. The emphasis on native-born Protestantism long remained a significant underpinning of the Republican Party in Maine even after the most virulent strain of anti-Catholicism, "Know-Nothingism", vanished from the scene. It helps explain why the Irish and many of the other immigrant groups that followed them in Maine were attracted to the Democratic Party.

5.30

5.29 *(facing page) Portland Company Locomotive Design, c. 1850. Founded in 1846, the Portland Company manufactured steam engines and other railroad equipment.*

5.30 *The 19-year-old Prince of Wales— later Edward VII—sailed from Portland in 1860 at the end of a Canadian tour. He was given a triumphal farewell, on what was to be his only American visit, with the streets so packed with militia companies the Prince is said to have complained, "Hurry, I'm cold!" One wellwisher tossed a bouquet so vigorously, she knocked the Prince's hat off just as he was boarding his ship.*

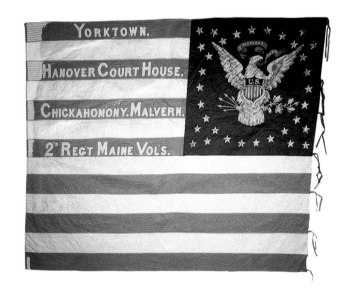

6.1

MAINE IN THE CIVIL WAR

❧ TO SAVE THE UNION

THE 1840S AND 1850S were years of change and turmoil in Maine. An economy once dependent on agriculture and fishing was seeing the beginnings of industrialization, notably the arrival of the railroads. Thanks to the heroic efforts of an entrepreneur named John A. Poor, a major railroad line had been run from Montreal to Portland, a city that for a brief time aspired to rival Boston. Other railroads linked Bangor, then the lumber capital of the country, to the rest of the state and nation. In the mid 1850s, Maine was also the wooden ship-building capital of the United States, and its famous clippers like the SNOW SQUALL and the RED JACKET were breaking speed records in the Atlantic and the Pacific. That golden era of sail ended when the Civil War brought the introduction of ironclads. Two of these were built at the Kittery Shipyard, which had also produced the more graceful looking tall ship KEARSARGE, a Yankee man-of-war that defeated the Confederate raider ALABAMA in a celebrated sea battle off the coast of France. More than 2,000 workers toiled at Kittery during the war, producing 26 warships in all. Another vital contribution of the transformed Maine economy to the North's war effort was gunpowder. The mills on the Presumpscot River at Gorham and Windham that produced it accounted for 5 percent of the entire powder supply used by the men in blue. Another dramatic statistic documenting Maine's part in the ultimate Union victory was that few other states produced a greater percentage of volunteers. Almost 80,000 Mainers served in the U.S. armed forces, the vast majority of them in the army, which suffered more than 7,000 casualties among its Maine troops in the war.

An acclaimed 1993 motion picture, *Gettysburg*, a four hour depiction of the epic battle, focuses a good deal of its attention on Colonel Joshua L. Chamberlain of the 20th Maine and the role his troops played in stopping a Confederate attempt to outflank the whole Federal army. Even in his lifetime,

❧

6.1 Civil War regimental flags, from the display in the Rotunda of the Maine State Capitol. Almost 73,000 Mainers served in the Union army and navy, the highest figure in proportion to population of any northern state.

〜

6.2 *Detail of the Civil War memorial to*

Maine's soldiers and sailors, erected in

Portland's Monument Square in 1888.

Maine's forces suffered more than 18,000

casualties in the effort to save the Union,

including 7,322 deaths.

Chamberlain's amazing maneuvers on Little Round Top were only belatedly recognized. His Congressional Medal of Honor was not awarded until 1893. And it was years after the battle that he was cited in the writings of Colonel William Oakes of the 15th Alabama Regiment, whose men had faced the 20th Maine. Of Chamberlain, Oakes wrote: "His skill and persistency and the great bravery of his men saved Little Round Top and the Army of the Potomac from defeat. Great events sometimes turn on comparatively small affairs."

Chamberlain's "small affair" was to keep the Southerners from capturing the key hill of Little Round Top on the Northern army's left flank. That Chamberlain's decisive action was at least appreciated by his superiors could be seen in the choice of the 20th Maine to receive surrender of the Army of Northern Virginia at Appomattox. Here, too, the Bowdoin College professor turned general found the right touch to put upon the event. As the defeated troops marched forward to lay down their guns and flags, Chamberlain had his men present arms in a tribute to their gallantry.

The 20th Maine was only one of 32 infantry regiments that Maine produced for the Union army. In addition, there were three cavalry regiments, one regiment of heavy artillery, seven battalions of mounted artillery, seven companies of sharpshooters, and thirty companies of unassigned infantry. They fought over a wide field, whether it was in famous battles like Gettysburg, Bull Run, Antietam, and Petersburg, or in lesser known campaigns like those in the South Carolina low country, Louisiana, and Texas.

A few Mainers achieved important commands, particularly General Oliver Otis Howard, a Bowdoin graduate and West Pointer from the tiny Androscoggin County town of Leeds. Howard is actually better known for his services after the war as head of the Freedmen's Bureau in the South than for his military efforts. Howard University was founded by him and he served as its first president.

On the civilian side, two distinguished Mainers made an impressive contribution to the war effort. Hannibal Hamlin, as Lincoln's first Vice President, was among those who pushed Lincoln to issue the Emancipation Proclamation. It has been claimed that Lincoln wanted Hamlin to remain as his Vice President but took no steps to help him secure the Republican nomination in 1864. Hamlin was ousted mostly through the machinations of Massachusetts' U.S. Senator Charles Sumner, a powerhouse among the "Radical," or very anti-Southern, Republicans. Ironically, they were to choose a Unionist Southerner, Andrew Johnson of Tennessee, to replace Hamlin. Moreover, Johnson turned out to be so completely inimical to their interests, that they tried to impeach him. Sumner's vendetta, paradoxically, was not against Hamlin but against Maine's veteran U.S. Senator William Pitt Fessenden. His Massachusetts colleague reasoned that if he could deny Hamlin the Vice Presidency, Hamlin would then run for the U.S. Senate and defeat Fessenden. That Machiavellian plot never achieved its purpose, since Hamlin, although out of office, never challenged Fessenden.

Fessenden—a tall, gaunt, quintessentially Yankee-looking lawyer—had found himself at the outbreak of the Civil War as chairman of the all-important Senate Finance Committee. Fessenden's job, therefore, was nothing less than to raise the money the North needed in order to carry on the war. From a government with a revenue of $25 million, Fessenden guided the U.S. to a point where it was expending $1 billion four years later.

In the critical summer of 1864, Fessenden was appointed Secretary of the Treasury by Lincoln. Reluctant to leave the Senate, he was eventually persuaded to take the post by the President, and in March 1865, after nine months at the job, he was allowed to leave to return to the Senate. As with General Howard, Fessenden's greatest fame came after the war when, despite the expectations of his fellow Radical Republicans, he cast the deciding vote against impeaching President Andrew Johnson.

6.2

～

6.3 *Among the Civil War artifacts in the Maine State Museum are an 1861 snare drum; an 1862 recruiting poster; the Congressional Medal of Honor awarded to Corporal M. L. Hansom, 19th Maine; a Tiffany & Co. sword presented to Colonel John D. Rust, 8th Maine, in 1864; Neal Dow's folding cot, when he was colonel of the 13th Maine; a cartridge box which belonged to Private Leonard Spearin of Gardiner; and a canteen carried by Horace C. Griffin of Holden, killed at age 21 at Spotsylvania in 1864.*

RICHMOND
TO BE TAKEN!
PEACE
To be Declared!

Probably the last chance to serve in the Volunteer Service!

A few more able-bodied men wanted to fill up the Company now on drill at Camp Jameson, Augusta, for the

16th Maine Regiment,

to be commanded by Capt. Daniel Marston. $2,00 premium, One month's pay, and a bounty of $25,00 in advance; also $75,00 and 160 acres of land, at the close of the service. Ample provisions made for all recruits at the Stoddard House, Farmington, and the Rail-road House, Phillips until taken into Camp.

Come one and all, and let us go and witness the dethronement of Jeff and his hirelings.

PAY AND SUBSISTENCE
to commence from the date of enlistment.

DANIEL MARSTON, Recruiting Officer.

Augusta, July 10 1862.

Farmington Chronicle Printing Establishment, No. 3, Main Street, Farmington, Me.

6.4

❧ CONFEDERATE ATTACKS ON MAINE

The last place in the Union where Rebel attacks might be expected to occur surely would have been Maine, then the northernmost of the states. Yet on several occasions, incidents of fighting and near fighting occurred in the state during the Civil War. One attack that was aborted without actual gunfire involved a raid across the border from Canada on the city of Calais. The aim of a group of Confederate conspirators assembled in New Brunswick was to rob the Calais Bank of a large supply of gold, which would be transferred to the Southern cause. The ringleader was William Collins, a Confederate captain who had family members living in St. John, New Brunswick. But through another family member, a Methodist minister living in York, Maine, the Union authorities were alerted to the plot and managed to infiltrate the raiders' ranks. Thus, on July 18, 1864, when four men in civilian clothes walked into the Calais Bank and went for their revolvers, the place bristled with the guns of the Federal agents who beat them to the draw. Collins and his accomplices were jailed as common bank robbers, but four months later the Irishman managed to escape from Thomaston Prison, reach Canada and return to continue fighting for the Confederacy.

In the most serious incident involving the Confederates and the Pine Tree State, a daring naval lieutenant named Charles W. Read was on a successful privateering venture in northern waters when he

❧

6.4 *Exterior of the Chamberlain House, Maine Street, Brunswick. The person in the doorway is believed to be General Joshua Lawrence Chamberlain, when he was president of Bowdoin College (1871-83).*

decided to capture a U.S. revenue cutter, the CALEB CUSHING, as she lay at anchor in Portland harbor. Read's plan was boldness itself. He would simply sail right past the guarding forts and seize the ship.

Read used a fishing boat he had captured to sneak by the guns, and from her he dispatched two small boats to put a boarding party on the CALEB CUSHING. The officer in charge of the cutter, ironically, was a Southerner who had joined the U.S. Navy, a native of Savannah, Georgia, who protested that he should not be handcuffed on that account when the invaders overpowered his men and himself.

The triumphant Confederates proceeded to ease the CALEB CUSHING out to sea. But its disappearance was noted, and the Yankees gave chase, led by the 460 ton steamship CHESAPEAKE. Firing broke out when the CHESAPEAKE bore down on the captured CALEB CUSHING. Read, realizing he was defeated, soon scuttled his prize, setting it afire and abandoning ship before she blew up. Later, the CHESAPEAKE was en route to Portland when a group of Confederate hijackers, including a brother of William Collins, took her over following a firefight in which one Yankee was killed. After coasting eastern Maine, the purloined steamer ended up in Nova Scotia, where the Canadian authorities impounded her and eventually returned the cutter back to the U.S.

A possible goad to Rebel action in the North was the existence of strong anti-war sentiment among much of the population. Despite its noted patriotism and exemplary record in supplying recruits, Maine, too, harbored a certain number of "Copperheads," as Southern sympathizers in the North were called. There was a major branch of the Maine Democratic Party that openly opposed the war, and in 1862 they even controlled the party convention. The editor of the *Bangor Democrat*, Marcellus Emery, was a leader of this group. He so incensed the locals that a mob of them broke into his newspaper office, destroyed his presses, and forced him to flee for his life. The antiwar Democrats still succeeded in running a candidate for Governor that year, but so did a rival bloc of prowar Democrats.

6.5

∾

6.5 *Colonel Joshua L. Chamberlain, 1863. As a result of novels, films, biographies, and television documentaries depicting his heroism at Little Round Top, during the battle of Gettysburg, Chamberlain was "rediscovered" in the late 20th-century as a major Civil War figure.*

6.6

A few years later, the Republican gubernatorial candidate Samuel Cony was able to squeeze out only an 18,000 vote margin over Bion Banbury, a noted Copperhead devoted to ending the conflict.

War weariness and revulsion over the draft became rampant in some parts of Maine. The most notorious outburst was the "Kingfield Riot," when the inhabitants prevented an army enrollment officer from delivering draft notices to local men. The Governor called up the Lewiston Light Infantry, primarily veterans of the 10th Maine, and they marched on Kingfield. Unlike the New York City draft riots where hundreds died, this contretemps ended in more typically benign Maine fashion. Attractive young women greeted the arriving infantrymen on the outskirts of Kingfield and escorted them to the center of town, where tables laden with food had been set out. The soldiers ate and flirted and in this convivial atmosphere, the draft notices were delivered and the law upheld.

∾ THE BATTLE FLAGS

The memory of Maine's role in the Civil War has been preserved, in part, in the faded banners of the Maine regiments now enclosed behind glass on the second floor rotunda of the State Capitol in Augusta. These regimental colors contain lettering that is difficult and in some cases impossible to decipher: the names of battles and the identities of units. Among them are obscure engagements that history has virtually forgotten: Kelly's Ford, North Anna, Aldie Station, Cane River, as well as places immortalized by heavy and strategic combat: Petersburg, Fredericksburg, Bull Run, Gettysburg. Flags of the 4th Maine Infantry, the 5th Maine Infantry, the 1st Maine Cavalry, and the 17th Maine Infantry, are also on display.

Confederate battle flags at one time were part of the collection in Augusta. But in the 1920s Governor Percival Baxter had them sent back to the South as a gesture of friendship and American unity.

These Civil War flags are simply the centerpiece of a larger collection that includes the banners of the Kennebec Guards, a militia unit from Gardiner formed at the time of Maine's statehood in 1820, plus colors from all of the wars in which Maine men and women fought up to the present. Some of them are of great significance, like the fragments of the flag of the 16th Maine, cut into pieces and

6.7a

6.7b

∿

6.6 (facing page) Senator William Pitt Fessenden. As Lincoln's secretary of the Treasury, Fessenden played a large role in financing the Northern war effort; as a U.S. Senator, he cast one of the deciding votes against President Andrew Johnson's impeachment.

∿

6.7a and 6.7b William Hall, "A New Year's Dinner at Camp Banks, Baton Rouge, 1863." Many Maine regiments served in the brutal campaigns in the lower Mississippi River and Red River valleys.

6.8

hidden at Gettysburg when in danger of capture and saved by some of the men who suffered captivity in Confederate prisons, thus fulfilling the boast that no Maine regiment ever surrendered its flag. Perhaps the most illustrious of all is another jewel of the collection—the battle flag of the 20th Maine.

Also in the second floor rotunda is a bronze plaque. Reflecting the sentimentality of a bygone era, it reproduces the poem written by a clerk in the Secretary of State's office who had overheard a visitor dismiss the nearby display as "nothing but flags." Indignant, Moses Owen reduced his irate feelings to ironic verse:

> *Nothing but flags—but simple flags*
> *Tattered and torn and hanging in rags...*
> *Nothing but flags—yet methinks at night*
> *They tell each other their tales of fright...*
> *Nothing but flags—yet they're bathed with tears.*
> *They tell of triumphs, of hopes, of fears...*
> *...They are sacred, pure and we see no stain*
> *On those dear loved flags at home again.*
> *Baptized in blood, our purest best.*
> *Tattered and torn, they're now at rest.*

The painstaking, expensive process of preserving this aspect of Maine's heritage is under way, led by the Save Maine's Colors campaign of the Friends of the Maine State Museum.

6.9

6.8 (facing page) Seventh Company, Unassigned Maine Infantry, at the State House, c. 1864.

6.9 General Oliver Otis Howard. More famous than Chamberlain in their own day, Howard is remembered now for his major role in establishing the Freedman's Bureau in the South and in encouraging former slaves to receive an education.

∾ THE GREAT PORTLAND FIRE

It was the first full year of peace and Portland, with the rest of the nation, was celebrating the Fourth of July. In the forenoon, the citizens of the Forest City had enjoyed a parade, and thousands of people were strolling in the streets. In the area now known as Deering Oaks, there was to be a balloon ascension. But in an omen of portending trouble, the balloon failed to take off and deflated.

6.10 *Edouard Manet was the most famous of several French painters who depicted the battle in 1864 between the Confederate raider* ALABAMA *and the Maine-built* U.S.S. KEARSARGE *off the French coast near Cherbourg. The* KEARSARGE *won.*

6.10

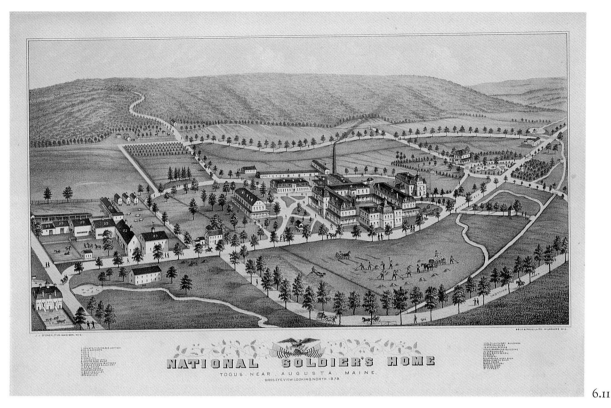

6.11 *A legacy of the Civil War: Togus Veterans Hospital, established in 1866, near Augusta, as the first institution in the country for disabled veterans. Built in the form a village, the facility is still in use.*

At Deguio and Dyer's boatbuilder's shop on Commercial Street, a pile of sawdust was set alight around 5 P.M., some claimed by a firecracker tossed by mischievous boys, others said by a lit cigar.

The unchecked flames, fanned by a strong southerly wind, reached another business establishment on Commercial Street. This was the Portland Sugar House, owned by the city's wealthiest entrepreneur, John Bundy Brown. It was actually a sugar refinery, housed in a huge brick building, the largest in town, and allegedly fireproof. The flames poured into it. Soon thick, black smoke from the burning sugar was casting a pall over Portland.

Scheduled for that evening had been a display of patriotic fireworks. Instead, cinders and sparks began appearing above the city's roofs. The conflagration swept into Gorham's Corner, a section inhabited by poor Irish immigrants living in small wooden shanties. The stock of fireworks in Day's Store exploded. Middle and Exchange Streets, the heart of the city's business center, became engulfed.

6.12 A reunion in 1889 of survivors of the 20th Maine at Little Round Top, Gettysburg. General Chamberlain is near the center. The veterans dedicated a marker at the spot where, on the second day of the battle in 1863, they held off a Confederate charge that could have turned the flank of the Union line.

With heat so fierce that bricks were burned into brilliant colors, the fire departments—Portland's meagre four steam pumpers and two hook and ladders, plus volunteer outfits that came from as far away as Boston—were virtually helpless. At 3 A.M., the fire was still burning.

As people fled their homes, they had to fear not only the terrible flames but a human scourge in the form of looters, robbers, and extortionist teamsters charging outrageous prices to haul persons and their goods to safety. The final toll of destruction was immense. Utterly demolished were all of the banks, eight of the churches, all of the newspaper offices, hundreds of homes and all public buildings, including City Hall. Portland's beautiful elms also suffered great damage.

If a bright spot existed, it was that the bank records had been salvaged unscathed. The *Portland Transcript* reported that "the Portland Savings Bank did not lose a dollar by the fire and will declare a dividend in November as usual."

Human interest stories were rife. One man saved his store by using barrels of brine for pickling beef to dampen the flames. He was down to two buckets of vinegar before the fire died out. Hannah Thurlo, aged 90, was led to safety from her home, which was spared; as an infant a few weeks old, she had been carried unharmed from the same site during Mowatt's bombardment in 1775 when the original family home had been destroyed. Because blowing up houses with gunpowder helped check the onrushing flames, Captain Frank L. Jones, lately of the 30th Maine, performed heroically by seizing a keg of explosives, dashing into a burning home on Pearl Street, setting off the fuse, and escaping before the blast created a clearing that kept all of the neighboring houses from burning.

Despite the devastation, only two persons were known to have died. Some burned bodies found were later ascertained to have been corpses already laid out in funeral homes.

The local jail caught fire. A man arrested for drunkenness, overlooked in the evacuation of prisoners, was discovered the next morning sound asleep on his cot, unaware of the blaze that had scorched the building around him.

To rebuild, Portland received help from communities all over Maine. Boston sent $25,000 in cash, and Newburyport $10,000, plus loads of provisions. New York City donated $100,000. More than $265,000 was received, a considerable sum in those days.

6.12

The *Transcript* had called their city "one of the most beautiful in the United States." A handsome new city did re-emerge. But it was quite different in style: Victorian and brick rather than Federal and wood. Some writers have maintained that more than styles changed as a result of the fire, that Portland somehow lost its confidence that it could overtake Boston as the leading port in New England. Whether this was ever a prospect is debatable. Yet it is fair to say that Portland was never the same again after 1866.

7.1

VICTORIAN MAINE

∾ THE REPUBLICAN ERA

THE VICTORY OF THE NORTH in the Civil War solidified the political power of the Republican Party throughout the country, although the ascendency was to be brief among the defeated states of the South. Maine had entered the GOP column even before Lincoln's victory in the election of 1860, and the Pine Tree State, with a few intermittent exceptions, was to stay squarely in that column until the 1970s. A number of the leaders of the 19th-century Republican Party were from Maine, none of greater stature than James G. Blaine—the GOP presidential standard bearer in 1884 who missed occupying the White House by the mere 1,040 plurality that lost him New York State—and Thomas Brackett Reed, "Czar Reed," the powerful, turn-of-the-century Speaker of the U.S. House of Representatives.

Had it not been for internal party politics played out at the GOP's 1864 convention, the President of the United States might have been a Maine man, too—Hannibal Hamlin. Those "Radical" Republicans who had ousted him as Vice President, led by Massachusetts Senator Charles Sumner, were soon to regret their action. The man they had foisted upon the country, Andrew Johnson, while seemingly as hostile towards the Southern aristocracy as they were, refused to go along with their programs, one of which was to enfranchise all of the ex-slaves and draw them into the Republican Party.

A major battleground between Johnson and his foes, which included Congressman Thaddeus Stevens of Pennsylvania, Senator Benjamin Wade of Ohio, and Maine's own Senator William Pitt Fessenden, centered on the institution created by Congress known as the Freedmen's Bureau, headed by Maine's General Oliver Otis Howard.

∾

7.1 *Frederic Edwin Church*, Mount Katahdin from Millinocket Camp, 1895. *Beginning with Thoreau's visit in 1846, Mount Katahdin represented for writers, artists, and naturalists a combination of wildness and grandeur to be found nowhere else in New England.*

7.2

7.3

7.2 and 7.3 What might look like a city after a bombardment is in fact the center of Portland after the devastating fire of 1866. The city was quickly rebuilt, in red brick and granite.

The Bureau had been created while Lincoln was still alive to help the freed slaves acquire land, receive an education, and participate in self government. In a major battle with President Johnson, who wanted to do away with it, Congress overrode his veto of the bill to extend its life. At the same time, a Joint Committee on Reconstruction, chaired by Fessenden, was setting up the framework to undo the President's unilateral action in allowing Southern states back quickly into the Union.

The decade between 1866 and 1876 was a time of turmoil and terrorism in the South. The Freedmen's Bureau, and the men who worked for it in the South—some from Maine like Eliphalet Whittlesey, a Bowdoin professor, who helped administer North Carolina—were constantly harassed, not infrequently at the instigation of President Johnson. Others like the war hero General Adelbert

7.4 *In 1871, President U. S. Grant met the Governor General of Canada in Bangor for the official opening of the European and North American Railway. To the left is the Bangor House, one of the most famous hotels in 19th-century Maine.*

Ames of Rockland, the Military Governor of Mississippi, were even physically threatened by the nightriding Ku Klux Klan that had sprung into being. In a memorable scene in Congress, Ames' father-in-law, ex-general and Congressman Benjamin Butler, illustrated the need for a law against the Klan by holding up a bloodstained shirt worn by a county superintendent in Mississippi who had been horse-whipped by the Klan. "Waving the bloody shirt" became a hallowed phrase in American political history, used to denominate the GOP's practice of refighting the Civil War in every election.

7.5

~

7.5 *Joshua L. Chamberlain as governor. A popu-*
lar war hero, Chamberlain served four terms
(1867-70) as an independent-minded Republican.

~

7.6 *(facing page) A banner from James G. Blaine's*
unsuccessful presidential campaign in 1884.

By 1869, Congressman James G. Blaine was the Speaker of the House. In the political infighting over the Military Reconstruction Act, the Radical Republican legislation that fastened a military government on the South, Blaine was able to soften this measure by declaring that a Southern state could escape its grasp by ratifying the 14th amendment and allowing blacks to vote.

The presidential election of 1876 allowed the South to undo Reconstruction entirely and without concessions to Blaine or anyone else. The election was very close, with the apparent winner Samuel Tilden, the Democrat, rather than Rutherford B. Hayes, the Republican. The electoral votes of three Southern states were needed by the GOP—South Carolina, Florida and Louisiana, where recounts had been requested. Deals were then concocted with Southern leaders, and in return for Republican victories in those three races, there was a withdrawal of Yankee troops, an end to military reconstruction and to guarantees of protection for Southern blacks. The GOP went to the White House and the old "Bourbons," the prewar establishment which had run the Confederacy, were once more ensconced in all of the state houses below the Mason-Dixon Line.

~ THE PLUMED WARRIOR

Rutherford B. Hayes, Governor of Ohio, had received the Republican nomination for President on the seventh ballot at the 1876 GOP convention in Cincinnati. The overall favorite to have won this nomination had been James G. Blaine of Maine. Affable, intelligent, an effective leader, Blaine was a powerhouse in the party, but a man around whom controversy continually swirled. First, there had been the Credit Mobilier scandal, when he was accused of using his position as Speaker to give favors to that organization's parent company, the Union Pacific Railroad, in return for 3,000 shares of stock. Having weathered the storm with glib and witty ripostes, he then, four years later, found himself in the midst of another railroad drama, this time involving the Little Rock and Fort Smith Line in Arkansas. The opposition newspapers focused on an item headlined "The Mulligan Letters," which were missives sent from Blaine to James Mulligan, a clerk for a stockbroker in Boston, that allegedly proved Blaine had been lying when he swore before a Congressional committee that he had never used $64,000 of the railroad's bonds as collateral for a Union Pacific loan he never had to pay back.

7.6

The press had a field day. Blaine physically confronted Mulligan at his hotel in Washington and managed to get the letters back into his possession. Blaine read them to a Congressional committee, demonstrating that they were innocuous, and ended by accusing the committee chair of suppressing a telegram from an Arkansas railroad official exonerating him. When the chair admitted he had received the telegram, the packed chamber went wild cheering Blaine.

7.7 The Blaine family at their Bar Harbor summer cottage with President Benjamin Harrison in 1889. What had been a small fishing and farming village on Mount Desert Island had become, after the Civil War, one of the most fashionable summer resorts on the East Coast.

7.7

A few weeks hence, the fateful convention was held. Blaine's nominating speech, delivered by Colonel Robert Ingersoll of Illinois, has gone into the annals of American political declamations, particularly for its opening lines, referring to the Mulligan episode, where "like an armed warrior, like a plumed knight, James G. Blaine marched down the halls of the American Congress and threw his shining lance full and fair against the brazen foreheads of the defamers of his country and the maligners of his honor." Ever afterward, in the media, Blaine was "the Plumed Knight."

Yet the nomination never became his. Blaine's diehard enemy, Senator Roscoe Conkling of New York, was consistently able to keep the Mainer from winning a majority of the delegates. On the sixth ballot, Blaine was a mere 71 votes shy. But on the seventh ballot, Conkling shifted enough votes to Hayes so that the Ohioan won by five votes.

How different American history might have been if Blaine had won the GOP nomination and the Presidency is an intriguing speculation. He later denounced the deal, "the Great Swap," that abandoned the Southern Republicans after the disputed election of 1876. Would the

7.8

7.8 The most famous—and most controversial—politician from Maine in the post-Civil War era, Blaine sought in vain to be president of the United States, a post which his national eminence in the Republican Party seemed to guarantee him. Frank Leslie's Illustrated Newspaper depicted him on the Blaine House front steps in 1884 addressing delegates to the convention.

7.9

7.9 *The Victorians' passion for household goods and gadgets is reflected in this selection of artifacts at the Maine State Museum from the years 1860-1920. (facing page) A self-propelling lawn sprinkler, c. 1880, Portland Sprinkler Company. A sunburst quilt, Lisbon, c. 1870, which descended through the Cushman family of Webster. An armoire, mid-19th century, found in Madawaska, which descended in the Hector Bourgoin family. (this page) A patchwork quilt with embroidered and painted squares, 1885, made for the Rev. F. L. Brooks, a circuit-riding minister, by the Harrington Methodist Society. A child's sled made by the Paris Manufacturing Company. A hooked rug of the "Waldoboro type," made c. 1914 by Sarah Engley as a wedding gift.*

7.10 *Stonecarvers at work on the "Statue of Faith" for the Plymouth Monument at the Hallowell Granite Company, c. 1890. Maine granite was shipped throughout the country for use in public buildings and monuments.*

7.10

No 236

resulting rule of Jim Crow in the South and its 20th-century heritage of civil rights battles have been as severe if Blaine had entered the White House in 1876? Conceivably not.

Eight years later, he came even closer to being elected President. His good friend James Garfield had won the Presidency in 1880, named Blaine his Secretary of State, and then was shot to death by a deranged assassin while riding with Blaine in a State Department carriage. With Chester A. Arthur, a protege of his arch foe Conkling as President, Blaine left government, wrote an autobiography, and came back to win the GOP nomination in 1884. Had it not been for the gratuitous "Rum, Romanism and Rebellion" speech of a fanatic Protestant minister that alienated many Catholics in New York State, Blaine would have won the election. (The Democrats, the preacher had suggested, were the party of hard drinkers, immigrant voters, and Southern sympathizers.) "The Lord sent us an ass in the shape of a preacher and a rainstorm to lessen our vote in New York" was the disgusted epitaph of one GOP politico. Ironically, Blaine, himself, had been born of an Irish Catholic mother, although raised as a Protestant.

7.11 *Thomas Brackett Reed, through the window of his Portland house. One of the most powerful speakers in the history of the U.S. House of Representatives, "Czar" Reed left his Congressional seat in 1899 in protest of U.S. colonialism in the Philippines and the Caribbean.*

Defeated by Grover Cleveland, he nevertheless went back into politics when Cleveland was beaten by Benjamin Harrison and once more served as Secretary of State. He devoted much of his foreign policy effort to establishing the first Pan-American Congress, a forerunner of the Organization of American States. In 1892, he made a final, futile attempt to gain the Republican Presidential nomination and died the following year.

One Pair
GREENWOOD'S
EAR PROTECTORS
Silk Velvet
For Well Dressed Men
Price 50 Cents.

FHS

CONY

The ATWOOD Patent
Variable   Tension

Size   yards

7.12

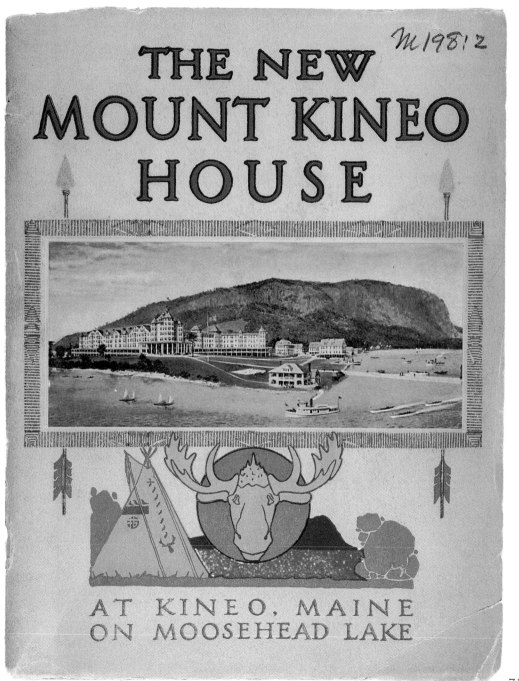

7.12 *(facing page) Maine as Vacationland produced a flood of leisure and sporting goods. Skis, made by the Paris Manufacturing Company, early 20th-century. A deer and moose horn chair, made by C. E. Fish of Jonesboro, c. 1920-30 ("a hunter's good luck chair"). A fishing reel, c. 1900, made by Leonard Atwood of South Farmington Falls. A pair of the famous ear muffs invented in 1873 by Chester Greenwood of Farmington. (December 21, the first day of winter, is officially Chester Greenwood Day in Maine.)*

7.13 *A 1911 pamphlet advertising the Mount Kineo House, a dramatically situated luxury resort toward the northern end of Moosehead Lake.*

7.13

7.14 *The Shaker Village at West Gloucester in the mid-19th-century. One of many dissident religious sects in 19th-century Maine, the Shakers are better known today for the much-admired simplicity of design of their traditional crafts, especially furniture. This is something of a distortion, for 19th-century Shakers lived in modest but typically Victorian clutter. The last active Shaker community in the country survives at Sabbathday Lake, as the West Gloucester village is now known.*

NOVITIATE ORDER, POLAND HILL.

EVERTS & PECK, PUBRS.   "SHAKER VILLAGE," VIEW FROM THE NORTH WEST, WEST GLOUCESTER, MAINE.   (Nº 2 CEMETERY.)

7.14

When James G. Blaine lost the Republican presidential nomination in 1876, there was a backlash against the GOP in Maine. Hayes carried the Pine Tree State, although by a sharply reduced margin.

A third party candidate also ran that year for Governor of Maine. He was a bearded, long-jawed farmer named Solon Chase, and he seemed like a joke, electioneering for something called the Greenback Party. His platform was to promote "easy money," and he illustrated his theme everywhere he went with a pair of oxen, referred to as "them steers," whose value, he said, the current reliance on "hard money" had reduced by half. Chase's numbers in that election seemed as ludicrous as he did: a mere 545 votes.

But, two years later, he almost beat Republican Congressman William Frye. Moreover, the Greenbackers that year elected two of Maine's five Congressmen. And the Republican Governor, Selden Connor, was denied a majority. Under Maine's election laws at the time, the race had to be settled by the Legislature.

An even more remarkable result of this election was that the Republicans had lost their control of the State House. The Greenbackers and Democrats, if they combined forces, could choose the Governor.

Combine they did. In the House they had a strong majority. Thus, only the names of a Democrat and a Greenbacker were sent to the Senate, which had a slight Republican majority. For the GOP, the lesser of two evils was the Democratic nominee, Alonzo Garcelon of Lewiston. In a state "where for 24 years, a Democrat had been looked upon as a natural curiosity or a perverted criminal," the iron grip of the Republicans was finally, albeit briefly, loosened.

7.15

∾

7.15 *Logging on the St. John River in the early 20th-century. From the 17th-century to the 1970s, the log drives each spring were a familiar sight on Maine's rivers.*

7.16 *The 1908 launching of the six-*
masted schooner EDWARD B.
WINSLOW *at the Percy & Small*
Shipyard at Bath in 1908. The largest
schooner in the world at the time, the
vessel was used in the coal trade until
destroyed by fire off the French coast in
1917. The crew of 14 was rescued.

7.17 *(facing page) Captain Frank*
Irving Pendleton of Searsport in
samurai costume, painted in Yokohama,
Japan, late 19th-century. Maine
built and Maine owned ships often
traded in the Pacific, guaranteeing,
among other things, an abundance
of East Asian decorative objects in
Maine coastal homes.

7.16

This was the first of several anomalies that occurred at intervals during the long Republican political reign in Maine. There were always particular reasons for the opposition's success: a third party; a short-term, emotional issue; a particular personality; a GOP split. The times when the Democrats achieved power never lasted long enough for that party to build a solid base of support.

∾ GUNS IN THE CAPITOL

The year was 1879. Once again, the race for Governor was three-sided. The incumbent, Democrat Alonzo Garcelon, fared poorly. The Republican, Daniel Davis—nicknamed Diarrhea Davis, as a result of rumors that he had faked an illness to escape combat in the Civil War—came in first but without a majority. The Greenbacker, Joseph Smith, placed second.

Once more, the election was thrown into the Legislature. But who controlled the Legislature? On the surface, it looked as if the Republicans did. Yet the Fusionists—the Democrats and Greenbackers—cried foul. They claimed that the GOP had bought votes and intimidated voters. Blaine, although in Washington, still controlled the Maine party, and there were estimates that he had pumped as much as $150,000 into the election. The ace in the hole for the Fusionists was that they still had control of the Governor and Council, who alone could certify the election returns.

One popular term for what happened next was "the Great Count Out." Republican candidates found themselves "counted out" for the most spurious of reasons—until a final total of 37 apparent GOP victors were denied their seats and another Fusion triumph was assured.

Back from Washington hurried James G. Blaine. "The Plumed Knight" quickly took charge. On November 17, 1879, he led a large crowd of Republicans into the State House and, confronting Governor Garcelon and the Council, demanded the returns be opened to public inspection. The Governor and his Council refused. On December 16, they issued certificates of election that guaranteed a Fusionist victory, both in the House and the Senate.

With the opening of the Legislature set for January 6, rumors of the use of armed force by Blaine and the Republicans swept the state. Governor Garcelon ordered guns and ammunition to be sent to Augusta from the arsenal at Bangor. En route, the wagonloads of weapons were intercepted by a mob and sent back.

7.17

7.18

7.19

Eventually, however, Garcelon did get his rifles and the State House became "Fort Garcelon," with 75 Fusionist paramilitary men guarding every door and window. Worried by the possibility of civil war, Garcelon called upon Maine's revered war hero, General Joshua Chamberlain, commander of the State Militia, to intervene. At the time, Chamberlain was also the president of Bowdoin College. With characteristic energy, he assumed command and ordered Blaine and his followers to keep away from the State House.

When the Fusionists let down their guard a few days later, the Republicans peacefully infiltrated and took physical possession of the House and Senate chambers. Appealed to by the Fusionists to eject them, Chamberlain replied that his only duty was to keep those chambers open to members. A Fusionist mob threatened the general's life. He calmly unbuttoned his coat and told the armed men to shoot him. A man in the crowd responded by threatening to kill anyone who harmed Chamberlain, and the tension broke.

In the following days, the atmosphere grew even more volatile. Chamberlain ordered a regiment to assemble at Gardiner, ready to march. On January 16, the State Supreme Court declared the Republicans had legally organized the Legislature. In a rump session, the Fusionists made Joseph Smith governor.

∽

7.18 *(facing page) Workers pause for a photograph to celebrate completion in 1893 of The Passaconaway on the Cape Neddick River, one of the many sprawling wooden hotels that lined Maine's coast at the close of the century.*

∽

7.19 *Despite the many social and economic changes the late 19th-century brought to Maine, many towns ended the century looking much as they had on the eve of the Civil War, as this 1894 panorama of East Machias suggests. Outmigration and abandonment of unproductive farms meant a population decline in many parts of the state.*

7.20 *Maine hotel life, old style: a late 19th-century view of the Robinson House (better known as the Jed Prouty Tavern), a venerable hostelry (1804) which is still in business in Bucksport.*

7.21 *Sarah Orne Jewett. In works like* Deephaven *and* The Country of the Pointed Firs, *Jewett depicted a pastoral Maine in peaceful, poetic decline, thereby helping to create an enduring image of the state as a place "outside of time." Her writing found parallels in the Colonial Revival architectural movement in southern Maine in the 1890s.*

7.22 *(facing page) Maine hotel life, new style: an early 20th-century view of the porch of the Poland Springs House, perhaps the state's best known resort at the time. Increased leisure for the middle classes and the arrival of the automobile boosted Maine's tourist trade.*

7.20

7.21

7.22

7.23

7.24a

7.24b

7.24c

On January 17, a Saturday, two Legislatures met in the State House. The Republicans elected Daniel Davis, and Chamberlain accepted the results.

That Saturday night, Davis tried to enter the Governor's office, found it locked, and had it pried open with a jackknife. The GOP stalwarts had to break into the Secretary of State's office, too, where they discovered that the official State Seal had been stolen by the previous Fusionist occupant.

When "Governor Smith" and the Fusionist legislators arrived at the State House on Monday, they were barred from entry by armed Augusta police. Next the militia appeared, summoned by Governor Davis. A Gatling gun, an early form of machine-gun, was posted at the main entrance. Intimidated, the Fusionists quietly withdrew.

The Republicans had regained their ascendancy. It would be many years before they had to surrender power again.

❧ THOMAS BRACKETT REED

As Speaker of the U.S. House of Representatives, Portland's Thomas Brackett Reed taught the nation a thing or two about power: the power of a glib tongue and a masterful manipulation of the English language, the power of an imposing physical presence (more than six feet of height and 300 pounds of heft), and the power of quick, bold, unexpected action and the sturdiness not to back down.

❧

7.23 *(facing page) Facade of the Maine State House, c. 1890. The structure was altered and enlarged in 1911.*

❧

7.24a, 7.24b *and* 7.24c *The seat of government: three views from the 1890s of the Maine State House—Executive Council Chamber, House, and Senate.*

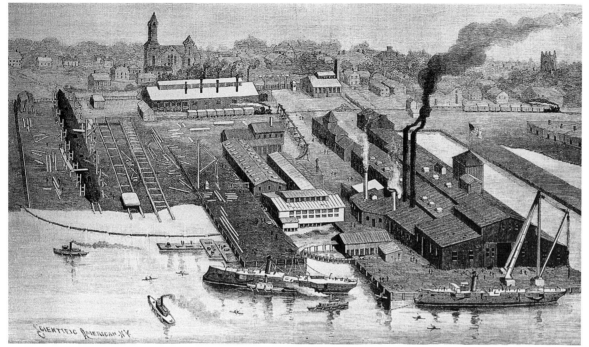

〰

7.25 The state's tradition of shipbuilding was preserved—and brought up to date—at the Bath Iron Works on the Kennebec, seen here in an 1893 issue of Scientific American. *Several of these brick buildings survive inside today's much larger shipyard complex.*

7.26

His rapier wit was much feared. When a pompous Democratic Congressman arose and declared sententiously, "Mr. Speaker, I would rather be right than President," Reed unhesitatingly shot back, "The gentleman need not worry. He will never be either."

After an equally withering sarcasm had cowed an obstreperous member, the Speaker elegantly remarked: "Having embedded that fly in the liquid amber of my remarks, I will proceed."

Reed's most famous moment came in 1890 during his second term as Speaker. He had been the Republican leader since 1885, having been nominated by William McKinley when the Republicans were in the minority and then having beaten McKinley for the post of Speaker in 1888. On January 29, 1890, the House assembled and, following a traditional practice of the opposition in those days, the Democrats refused to answer a roll call, thereby depriving the body of a quorum and holding up all business. Reed was three votes shy of the quorum he needed. But rather than give in to this manoeuver, he unexpectedly ordered: "The Chair directs the Clerk to record the names of the following members present and refusing to vote." He read off the names of the Democrats. They were apoplectic,

ISRAELSON & MARX.

7.27 *Israelson & Marx Storefront, Rumford, c. 1895. Maine had a small Jewish community in the late 19th-century, much of it settled in Portland, Bangor, and Calais. As this view from a Rumford promotional booklet suggests, some of its members prospered in retail trades.*

shouting in protest that he couldn't do what he was doing; meanwhile, the Republicans cheered madly. Finally, calling out the name of McCready of Kentucky, Reed was confronted with the statement: "I deny your right, Mr. Speaker, to count me as present." In the silence that ensued, Reed waited until all eyes were upon him and then challenged McCready: "The Chair is making a statement of fact that the gentleman is present. Does he deny it?" The session ended with Reed's definitive ruling that "there is a quorum present within the meaning of the Constitution."

His ruling was challenged. He was called a "Czar," and a "tyrant." But the man from Portland prevailed, sustained by the House's Rules Committee, whose new set of rules following the crisis became forever afterward known as "Reed's Rules."

"Czar" Reed had achieved national celebrity. He was often mentioned as a presidential possibility.

7.28

7.29

∾

7.28 *Lewiston Telephone Exchange, 1889.*

The telephone joined the electric light, the motor car, and improved sanitation as hall-marks of modernity in everyday Maine life.

In 1895, he announced his candidacy. His chief rival was William McKinley. His strong sense of personal rectitude, his sarcasm and wit, his unwillingness to play political games or curry favor in order to attract campaign funds left him at a distinct disadvantage when up against McKinley's manager, the veteran Ohio political boss, Mark Hanna. Despite strong support from Teddy Roosevelt and Senator Henry Cabot Lodge, Reed was swamped at the convention.

Reed's friendship with Roosevelt and Lodge was personal, not ideological, since they were expansionists and he was an active member of the Anti-Imperialist League, opposed to overseas adventures like the Spanish-American War and the annexation of the Phillipines as an American colony. Reed resigned from Congress rather than support the jingoistic policies favored by a majority of his own party.

A contemporary called him "the ablest running debater the American people ever saw." Another proclaimed him, "the greatest parliamentary leader of his time…far and away the most brilliant figure in American politics." Historian Barbara Tuchman characterized the illustrious Speaker from Portland as "uncompromising to the end, a lonely specimen of an uncommon kind, the Independent Man."

7.30

7.29 *(facing page) The jewelry and cigarette box department of the Brunswick Paper Box Company, c. 1901. Like Maine's other manufacturing towns, Brunswick by the turn of the century had a large Franco-American labor force which had moved south from the declining farm villages of Quebec in search of work. By the end of the 20th-century, about 40 percent of the state's population was of French Canadian descent.*

7.30 *Moving house in Brunswick, c. 1900. The Italianate "captain's house," which today houses the Delta Sigma Society at Bowdoin College, was moved across town on logs by oxen—a familiar technique for relocating timber-framed houses in 19th-century Maine. The arrival of the train somewhat complicated this particular effort, however.*

8.1

MODERN TIMES

∾ PAPER, POWER, AND TRAINS

EANWHILE, a number of economic developments were taking place that helped to enhance Republican influence in the state. Paper companies, power companies, and railroads were becoming major players on the political scene.

Ironically, the paper company that epitomized the industry's clout in the state—the Great Northern Paper Company, in Millinocket—was started by Democrats. To be sure, they were wealthy Democrats, men like William C. Whitney, his brother-in-law Colonel Oliver H. Payne, Daniel Lamont, and Pierpont Morgan, all friends of President Grover Cleveland. Originally, their investment in Maine paper production had been at a plant in Madison; they were then persuaded to place their money in a bigger venture that involved nothing less than the creation of a whole new industrial town in the Maine wilderness.

The entrepreneur who put this package together was a New Jerseyan named Garrett Schenck, who had been a manager at the International Paper Company mill in Rumford. With the completion of the Bangor and Aroostook Railroad's line from Old Town to Houlton in 1892, the dream of a Bangor real estate man, Charles Mullen, to build a major paper mill on property near Millinocket Stream became feasible. Schenck's involvement made the project a reality. In 1899, the Maine Legislature granted a charter for the Great Northern Paper Company.

A entire city was built from scratch. For the first time, foreign born laborers were introduced to northern Maine on a large scale. Some were "Polacks," a generic term that lumped together Poles, Lithuanians, Finns, Hungarians, Latvians, Estonians, and Czechs. But the largest group was Italian, so much so that the community of jerry-built shacks that sprang up overnight to house the workers was soon dubbed "Little Italy." Labor contractors called "padrones" recruited their countrymen in southern New England.

∾

8.1 *N. C. Wyeth,* Dark Harbor Fishermen, *1943. While not as famous an artist as his son and grandson, N. C. Wyeth was one of the most popular book illustrators of his day and established the Wyeth family's strong artistic connection with the Maine coast.*

8.2

8.3

On March 16, 1901, Millinocket, "the miracle city in the wilderness," became Maine's 467th town, home of the world's largest newsprint mill. Great Northern, spreading its operations to other towns and owning hundreds of thousands of acres of timberland, loomed on the Maine political scene with its lobbyists as a giant among giants. Schenck, always a strong Republican, helped to see that the GOP's hegemony in Maine was maintained.

Another powerful industrialist was Walter Wyman, the founder of the Central Maine Power Company. In 1910, a state senator referred to the company as an "octopus," swallowing up other power companies left and right. It had begun as the Messalonskee Electric Company, a small firm in the greater Waterville area. Wyman had bought this company, which then served only Oakland and Belgrade, for $4,500. Next, he moved into Waterville. In 1910 he had expanded enough to change the name to the Central Maine Power Company. Today, it covers all of southern and most of central Maine until it reaches the boundaries of the Bangor Hydro-Electric Company. CMP, as it is popularly known, is by far the biggest electric utility in the state. For many years, it was one of the most powerful political forces, again closely allied with the dominant Republican Party for much of this century.

The Maine Central Railroad completes this trio of prime influences from the economic sector on the politics of the state. The line had been organized in 1862. A battle in the Legislature fomented by rival railroads, taking the form of a fight over what size gauge to use for rails, led the Maine Central to realize early on the value of political support. Among its first presidents were two Republican ex-Governors, Anson P. Morrill and Abner Coburn.

8.4

⌇

8.2 *(facing page, above) Millinocket—"the*

magic city in the wilderness"—sprang up

almost overnight in 1900 to house the workers

of the Great Northern Paper Company's new

mill, which at the time was the world's largest.

Mount Katahdin can be seen in the background.

⌇

8.3 *(facing page, below) The dedication in 1931*

of Central Maine Power's Wyman Dam, in

Moscow, Maine, named in honor of the compa-

ny's founder, Walter S. Wyman. For much of the

1920s he was the most powerful and politically

influential business leader in the state.

Like the Central Maine Power Company, the Maine Central absorbed other companies, beginning in 1870 with its main rival, the Kennebec and Portland. Soon after came John A. Poor's European
and North American Railway, which ran to the Canadian border. President Ulysses S. Grant voyaged
in person to the tiny frontier town of Vanceboro to attend the ceremonies celebrating the linkage. The
Portland and Rumford Falls Railway Company, which had been started by Hugh Chisholm, the organizer of the International Paper Company, was another acquisition.

⌇

8.4 *A review of Maine troops in Brunswick in*

1918. More than 35,000 Mainers fought in

World War I, with more than 2,000 casualties,

including 1,073 deaths.

8.5

Before long, too, the Maine Central was taking advantage of Maine's developing tourist trade. Affluent families "from away" rode to elegant resorts on the company's trains or on the company's steamships. Some of the most elegant of the resorts where they stayed for the summer "season," like the Mount Kineo House on Moosehead Lake or the Samoset Hotel at Rockland, were also owned by the Maine Central.

The last half of the 19th-century and the early years of the 20th. saw Maine transformed. Its resources—forests, rivers, lakes, coastline—were subjected to various economic uses of far greater intensity than ever before. Paper, power, travel, tourism—a pattern of development that still exists as a basic underpinning of Maine's modern economy—had reshaped the once largely rural, agrarian state.

∾ MODERN MAINE TAKES SHAPE

The transformation of Maine's economy from its basic reliance on agriculture and fishing was not accepted without resistance. The changes wrought by new life styles associated with new industries were felt and resented, often explicitly but perhaps on occasion subliminally. No historian has pinpointed exactly when "Down East humor" was born, that reputed distillation of Maine character, aimed for the most part at visitors "from away" and their foolish questions. Yet the growth of the tourist industry in the state had to have played a large role. The first major hotel, the Marshall House in York Harbor, was built in 1871, the inspiration of a transplanted Englishman, but summer boarders had been appearing decades earlier. Along the coast, where the shipbuilding and shipping trades had declined, the newcomers and their money were welcome. The clash of cultures nevertheless left its mark, often as a kindly spoof.

Toward other intruders, Mainers were not so kind, at least at first. The Irish who came to Bangor to work in lumbering or to Portland as laborers to build the railroads before the Civil War sparked the excesses of the "Know Nothing" era, with raw anti-Catholicism played out in all its ugliness. Indeed, Bangor converted from a town form of government to a city government in 1838 after a meeting house used as a Catholic church was torched by a mob; responsible citizens had concluded that a selectmen-town meeting arrangement hadn't been strong enough to prevent the outrage.

∾

8.5 *Charles Woodbury,* Ogunquit Beach House with Lady and Dog, 1912. *In the early 20th-century, Ogunquit attracted a summer colony of artists and collectors, attracted to its broad sandy beaches and "quaint" fishermen's coves.*

8.6

~

8.6 *The sinking of the Maine built*
DOROTHY B. BARRETT *by a German*
U-boat off the New Jersey coast in 1918.
The photograph was taken by the captain's
son from their lifeboat.

The mass migration of the French-Canadians to Maine began in the 1870s. Ex-farmers from the impoverished villages of Quebec came in droves to toil in the textile mills that had sprung up alongside Maine's rivers. The "Know Nothings" were gone by this time, but the prejudice the Quebecers experienced was just as palpable, if perhaps less violent. Nor was it only the native Yankees whose scorn the French had to face. Their co-religionists, the Irish Catholics who had preceded them by several decades, were almost equally as hostile at the start.

Several cities of Maine to this day have Franco-American majorities or substantial minorities. Lewiston, Biddeford, Sanford, Waterville, Brunswick, are still centers for the largest non-Anglo population group in the state, even though the textile mills and shoe shops where their immigrant forebears worked have largely disappeared.

Water power, in use in Maine for economic purposes since the first colonists arrived, was long a major resource, and its control often became a political battleground. Sometimes clashing economic interests caused the tension. By 1907, there was a battle royal, a harbinger of others to come, when hotelman Edward P. Ricker and his brothers, the proprietors of the famed Poland Springs resort, championed tourism over electricity in defeating the Union Water Power Company's attempt to draw down the Rangeley Lakes. Eventually, this conflict was expressed in pithy Maine language as the choice between "payrolls or pickerel."

⌘ PERCIVAL BAXTER

Even before Maine's modern economic development began, there were those in the state, as in the nation, ideologically opposed to public "internal improvements." For example, in 1836, an act to create a geological survey for Maine with the aim of discovering exploitable minerals was barely passed in Augusta and, within three years, its funding withdrawn. Hostility to canals and railroads was equally as strong. Call it, if you will, the natural parsimony of a legislature dominated by hardscrabble farmers. But also call it a kind of Jeffersonianism, a belief that the ideal citizen was the independent yeoman, working in agriculture, fishing or "mechanics," which meant small scale handwork like carpentry or blacksmithing.

Percival Proctor Baxter did not begin his political career in Maine as an environmentalist. He had not chosen "pickerel" over "payrolls," although he loved to fish in Maine lakes. His wealthy father had made his initial money in the canning business, and had then increased the family fortune by extensive and judicious real estate investments, mostly in Portland. Young Percival, one of eight children, born to the second of James Phinney Baxter's wives, was brought up amid great wealth. Having retired from business, James Phinney Baxter entered politics and was elected six times Mayor of Portland. He was also a noted philanthropist and dedicated amateur historian, who travelled to England to find ancient records pertaining to Maine, while enrolling his youngest son Percy in an exclusive British "public" (i.e., private) school.

The Mayor's son went on to Bowdoin, Harvard Law School, and then, not surprisingly, to the Legislature. A Republican like his father, strong for temperance and other GOP issues, he ran some of his father's campaigns and in 1904, entered the lists himself as a candidate for the House seat from a Portland that was not always in his party's pocket. Two years later, Percy found this out the hard way when he was defeated for reelection.

In all, he was to win election to five terms in Augusta, three in the House and two in the Senate, suffering two defeats in-between. In his last term, he was chosen Senate President, and unkind tongues whispered that party bosses had engineered his victory to "kick him upstairs" and quell an independent spirit who had been wreaking havoc with the business as usual approach of the Old Guard.

8.7

⌘

8.7 *Governor Percival P. Baxter, donor of Baxter State Park and champion of the Fernald Law of 1909, prohibiting the export of hydroelectric power from the state.*

8.8

8.9

~

8.8 *Edwin Arlington Robinson. Born at Head Tide and raised in Gardiner—the "Tilbury Town" of his poetry—Robinson won the Pulitzer Prize in 1921, 1924, and 1928.*

Percy Baxter had dared to take on, again and again, those pillars of the Republican Party, the power and paper interests.

The biggest fuss he made was about the use of "the people's white coal"—running water in rivers and streams. Two principles were his guiding lights: 1) Maine's water power should not be exploited for the benefit of out-of-state speculators (in other words, it should not be used to generate electricity that would be sent beyond Maine's borders, a tenet he established in law in 1909); 2) Companies using Maine's waters should pay for the public rights on which they were making a profit.

In the latter instance, Baxter was following a tradition within the Republican Party established by Theodore Roosevelt and his close associate Gifford Pinchot, America's first forester, who had vigorously advocated that the country's resources were no longer simply to be given away for nothing. Another Roosevelt-Pinchot theme—conservation of resources—also struck a chord in Baxter.

8.9 *(facing page) Marsden Hartley. The greatest Maine born painter yet to appear, Hartley grew up in Lewiston then spent many years in Europe and New York. He returned to Maine later in life, much misunderstood as a Modernist artist but drawn to the state's mountains, coast, and working people.*

8.10 *The arrival of summer rusticators and other visitors created a new market for Native American crafts, including birch bark canoes and a variety of domestic goods. Traditional materials—bark, beads, porcupine quills, ash splints, sweetgrass—were incorporated into souvenirs for the tourist trade and furnishings for summer cottages.*

8.10

8.11

∾

8.11 *Edna St. Vincent Millay. "Discovered" as a poet in Camden—whose landscape provided the setting for her most famous poem, Renascence—Millay spent her most productive years in Greenwich Village but often returned to coastal Maine. She won the Pulitzer Prize in 1922.*

8.12

8.13

The *Portland Press Herald* wrote in 1927: "The silliest proposal ever made to a legislature was that of Governor Baxter who advocated the state's buying Mount Katahdin and creating a State Park." This may have been an idea of Baxter's as early as 1903. In his later campaigns for State Senate, a "Mount Katahdin Park" was prominently featured in his advertisements. On the last day of January 1921, Senate President Baxter learned the stunning news that the elected Governor, Frederick Parkhurst, had suddenly died. Under Maine law, he was now the Governor. If the GOP Old Guard had thought they were elevating Percy Baxter to safe oblivion, they now had a shock in store.

Through two tumultuous terms, Baxter served as Maine's Governor. He fought the power and paper companies to a standstill over water power "giveaways." While incurring the epithet of "socialist," he proved to be one of the most tightfisted fiscal conservatives ever to be Maine's chief executive, actually lowering the state budget and vetoing almost every money bill in sight.

8.12 *(facing page, above) The new hydroelectric dams provided not only power to light homes, factories, and streets but also a new mode of transportation—electric trolleys, such as these on a Bangor street c. 1911. Soon a network of trolley lines connected Maine towns and resorts.*

∿

8.13 *(facing page, below) Movie advertisement, Bangor, c. 1916. By World War I, virtually every Maine town had a place to show motion pictures, even if it consisted of only a bare wall and a projector. A number of early filmmakers also used Maine as a location.*

∿

8.14 *This candid shot on an Augusta street by an unidentified amateur conveys not only the popularity of the camera in turn-of-the-century America but also a particular moment in the history of transportation—an age when horse, train, and car could share the same scene.*

MODERN TIMES

159

8.15

∾

8.15 *The first round the world flight touched down in Casco Bay at Mere Point in 1924—its first landing on American soil—and was greeted by a flotilla of power boats and canoes.*

His one significant failure as Governor was to achieve his cherished Mount Katahdin Park. In this regard, the legislature proved itself exceedingly tightfisted and also conducive to the objections of the Great Northern Paper Company, which owned the land where Maine's highest mountain is located.

Leaving office and never returning to elected public service after a failed attempt to win the Republican nomination for U.S. Senate in 1927, Baxter set about to buy the land with his own money. Schenck, the crusty founder of the paper industry giant that owned it, was his biggest obstacle. Schenck had helped bankroll Baxter's opponent in the 1927 primary and had no sympathy for a Katahdin Park. After he died in 1928, his successors showed more interest, particularly the new president of Great Northern, William A. Whitcomb, who actually admired Percy for "having the courage of his convictions." The first sale to Baxter occurred in 1930. It gave him a three-eighths undivided interest in the northern two-thirds of the township that contained Katahdin. It was this piece of property that Baxter deeded over to the state in 1931 with the proviso that it be kept "forever wild." To this initial plot of 5,760 acres, he was eventually to add almost 200,000 more over a period of 30 years, all bought with his own money and generously donated to the people of Maine.

∾ACADIA

Baxter State Park, as Percival Baxter's creation came to be named by a grateful Legislature, had not been the only effort to conserve environmentally important land in Maine. Perhaps serving as a model was the twenty seven year struggle to create Acadia National Park, the only national park at the time east of the Mississippi and today one of the most visited. Here, too, a single-minded individual, a Boston Brahmin and summer visitor, George Bucknam Dorr, played a key role, even using some of his own money to acquire property. Unlike Baxter, he had financial help from his well-heeled friends and neighbors on Mount Desert Island and, in what would have been anathema to Baxter, he ultimately turned to the Federal government for support. The town where Dorr had his summer home when he started this project was then called Eden. Today, it is known as Bar Harbor. Even in the late 20th-century, it remains the symbol of a life style possible in an era before the income tax when a few could be fabulously rich and exclusive, living in an enclave apparently safe from the assaults of modernity. It was characteristic that John D. Rockefeller could seek to preserve his carriage roads around Seal Harbor by having automobiles banned in the region. Dorr's magnificent obsession was to save as much of that world's scenic value as possible for posterity, even at the cost of opening it to everyone.

8.16

∾

8.16 *While not as violent as their Southern models, Maine's Ku Klux Klan—seen here parading hooded in Gardiner—were a threatening sight in the 1920s for anyone who was not a white Protestant. The Klan tapped into the same nativist vein that had inspired the anti-Irish agitation of the 1840s, though the new targets were more likely French Canadian.*

∾ NATIVISM AND THE KLAN

By the time George Bucknam Dorr received the final designation for his park in 1928, a very different kind of "revolt" against modernity had been affecting Maine for at least three years. In 1925, it was estimated that there were more than 150,000 members of the Ku Klux Klan in the Pine Tree State. Nationwide, this terrorist organization, begun in Tennessee after the Civil War to supress the newly freed blacks, had been revived in the early 20th-century and claimed 9 million members. Certainly, the rise of the Klan in Maine had a religious and nativist context; with few blacks or Jews in the state, its chief bias was anti-Catholic. These latter-day Know-Nothings marched in their sheets, burned their crosses, and entered politics while crying out against the growing numbers of Catholics and "foreigners" in the state. In the prejudiced words of their King Kleagle, F. Eugene Farnsworth:

8.17

8.18

8.17 and 8.18 After two generations of campaigning

and years of legislative debate, Maine women finally

won the right to vote in 1920 with the passage of the

Nineteenth Amendment. Because Maine then voted in

September, ahead of the rest of the country, Maine

women became the first in the country to cast their

hard won votes in a national election.

I can show you the tombstones of the murderers of our Presidents—and they're not in Protestant cemeteries...This is not an Italian nation, this not an Irish nation, and this is not a Catholic nation, it has always been and always will be a Protestant nation.

The public figure most opposed to them was Governor Baxter. It was not generally known that his older sister Emily had converted to Catholicism before dying relatively young in 1921. Yet Baxter's crusade against the Klan was not merely personal. Throughout his political career, he had shown a tolerance unusual for those times. He appointed the first Jewish person to public office in Maine; he even defended the Japanese as a people he admired and, in an act of unusual courage, was the only American governor who refused to sign a resolution calling for an end to Chinese immigration in California. Earlier, he had led a legislative campaign for women's suffrage in Maine even before the reform became an amendment to the U.S. Constitution.

Baxter's perserverance in attacking the Klan paid off. His plea to his fellow GOP party members for an "old-time Republicanism where no distinction of Catholics, Protestants, Hebrews or Klansmen was ever thought of" eventually reflected the majority opinion. Almost as quickly as it had arisen, the hate group dwindled. From perhaps 150,000 members it had shrunk, by 1931, to 188 at its last public meeting in Maine.

℘ THE WOMAN SUFFRAGE MOVEMENT

In the early 1980s, the Maine Legislature ignited a brief spark of national attention by passing a resolve for "Chester Greenwood Day," honoring a Farmington native, the inventor of ear muffs, on the 100th anniversary of his birth. Everyone thought it was amusing to commemorate Greenwood's useful but hardly portentous

8.19

creation (he also invented shock absorbers). But no one thought to smirk or smile at the mention of his wife, Isobel Whittier Greenwood. That's because practically no one remembered her or knew that she had been a leader in the state's suffrage movement, an organizer of the Franklin County Equal Suffrage Association in 1906, and the donor of the Greenwood Collection on Woman Suffrage to the University of Maine's Fogler Library in Orono.

The struggle of Maine women to be allowed to vote was an epic battle, lasting almost 70 years. As early as 1854, Susan B. Anthony spoke in Bangor. The first organized group came together in Rockland in 1868, thanks to the work of Lavinia and Mary Snow. Two years later, the women were intrepid enough to present suffrage petitions to the Legislature. In the polite language of the lawmakers, still in use today, their sponsors were given "leave to withdraw" their petitions, a popular euphemism for killing a measure.

℘

8.19 *Female workers with their foreman, Cabot Mill, Brunswick, c. 1925. Women were in much demand as laborers in Maine's textile mills; they were considered reliable, docile, and dexterous.*

8.20

∾

8.20 *Main Street of the now "drowned village" of Flagstaff on the Dead River in northern Maine, a casualty of the need to dam rivers for hydroelectric power. The town was abandoned and flooded in 1950.*

Three years after that, suffragettes held a convention in Augusta and formed a statewide organization. The keynote speaker was Julia Ward Howe, the author of "The Battle Hymn of the Republic." (Her daughter, Laura Howe Richards, would later become a Pulitzer Prize winning author and important citizen of Gardiner.) The Legislature was at least paying some attention to this new political movement; members of its Judiciary Committee were there as observers. The movement spread. By the turn of the century, there were local suffrage leagues in Augusta, Saco, Waterville, Hampden, Old Orchard, Skowhegan, Auburn and Machias. Left $2,000 by Hadassah Herrick of Harmony, the Maine branch of the American National Woman Suffrage Association intensified its activity, despite constant setbacks, pointing out that 15,000 women in the state paid taxes and thus were suffering taxation without representation.

They picked up outside support: the National Grange in 1887, the Maine Grange in 1902, the Maine Federation of Labor in 1906. Important politicians in the dominant Republican Party swung their way—Percival Baxter and Ralph Owen Brewster, both future Governors, and Guy P. Gannett, newspaper tycoon and GOP powerhouse. In 1914, a Men's Equal Suffrage League was formed. Opposition from Maine Democrats was strong, however, for the cause of women's suffrage was linked in the public mind with the campaign for total prohibition.

In 1917, there was action on several fronts. The Maine Legislature, following a precedent set by other states, passed an amendment to its own constitution allowing women to vote. Percival Baxter led the fight in the House and Guy P. Gannett in the Senate. On the day of the vote, supporters and opponents paraded in the halls, identifying themselves by the yellow jonquils or red roses they wore.

The Republicans had a woman suffrage plank in both their state and national platforms; the Democrats only on the national level. In the House debate, the Democratic leader, Rep. Edward Murray of Bangor, asked for time to caucus his members. He was given a day. Then, the votes were taken. Baxter won his fight by a resounding 113 to 35. Gannett did even better, 35 to 0, in the Senate.

But amendments to the state constitution have to go to the people for their approval. The vote in September 1917 was a disappointment, with suffrage losing by a 2 to 1 margin.

The next opportunity came after Congress passed the 19th Amendment. The ratification debate was led by Baxter in the House. He drew flashes of anger from one member, Rep. Benedict Maher of Augusta, when he likened women's lack of a vote to slavery for blacks. Once again, he won on the issue but it was a squeaker, 72 to 68. The closeness of the vote did not bode well when the antisuffrage forces tried to mobilize against what had been done. They went to court but failed to obtain a ruling that the law was unconstitutional. Next, they moved for a statewide referendum, remembering the results of the previous one.

On August 26, 1920, enough states had ratified the amendment giving voting rights to women for it to become the law of the land. Less than three weeks later, on September 13, Maine voters went to the polls. They gave an overwhelming endorsement to woman suffrage, 88,080 to 30,462. The stage was set for full political participation by women in Maine, even though the process would take time and met much resistance.

∾ DORA PINKHAM

The first woman legislator in Maine was a one-time school teacher elected to the House in 1922 for the northernmost community of Fort Kent. Unlike many of her constituents, she was not of French-Acadian heritage, and she was a Republican. Dora Pinkham's politics, however, were hardly those of the conservative wing of her party. Her first speech in the House in 1923 was a blast against an amendment to the State Constitution to prohibit any form of aid to "sectarian schools"—a measure labeled anti-Catholic because it was aimed at parochial schools. Pinkham attacked it for "fanning the flames of fanaticism." The resolve, needing a two-thirds vote, failed on final enactment.

8.21

∾

8.21 *Dora Pinkham, of Fort Kent, who became the state's first woman legislator upon her election to the Maine House of Representatives in 1922.*

8.22

∾

8.22 *Biddeford's dense cluster of 19th-century red-brick textile mills and factories could serve as a symbol of the "other" Maine of the Early Modern Age—not a pastoral vacationland, but a hardworking industrial state, with a large Franco-American population.*

Next, she took on the Governor himself, who was none other than Percival Baxter. That he had been helpful if not instrumental in her having attained the right to be where she was and that he was the first Maine Governor ever to appoint women to public positions did not intimidate her in the least. When he vetoed her bill for the erection of a State of Maine building at the Eastern States Exposition in Springfield, Mass., she led the charge that overrode his objections, which were based on the fact that he did not want to spend any money.

Baxter's next veto of a bill of hers was also based in part on his penchant for penny-pinching. But, in addition, he had an ideological objection—he was utterly opposed to the state's acceptance of any Federal money—and Pinkham's bill would have had Maine receive funds for assisting with the health needs of indigent mothers and children. The bill had been passed with considerable difficulty. To receive $25,000 in Federal funds, Maine would have had to match them. Pinkham pointed out that 42 other states had already done so and that Maine's infant mortality rate, while it had dropped from 102 per 1,000 births, was still 76 per 1,000, the 28th in the nation (today, it is 7 per 1,000).

The American Medical Association was opposed on the grounds that obstetrics would be taken out of the hands of doctors and given over to state health departments. It was clear that Pinkham's heart was really in this bill as she eloquently countered such objections. She prevailed in the House by a seven vote margin. But Baxter's veto was sustained. To his contention that defeat of the bill would return Maine "to the fundamental doctrine that the State is sovereign and will brook no interference in its internal affairs," she exploded: "That sounds almost like a declaration of Civil War. We once had a war to decide the same question of states rights."

Her stint in the House was followed by two terms in the Senate, representing Aroostook County. From the first, she had served notice that she was not to be considered a token female whose job was to be seen and not heard. Throughout her career, she fought as hard and effectively as any of her male counterparts and more so than many.

Sentiments expressing her impact on this previously all male institution surfaced toward the end of her first term. In the type of ceremony beloved of the House, which can be very sentimental at times, bouquets of roses were given to the wives of men prominent in the running of the body. After roses had been presented with appropriate statements, including homemade poetry, to the wives of the clerk, the assistant clerk, and the Speaker, the lawmakers offered flowers for the first time in their history to one of their own members.

Rep. Bernard Archibald of Houlton presented the flowers and he said:

"How often we have heard it said that woman should be kept in her place...we may perhaps find it somewhat easier to keep her in her place because of necessity from now on the place that she may occupy will have no bound. She has had a large family on her hands here and I feel that under her careful guidance and supervision...we have been held in check by the respect that we all owe her."

It remained for Percival Baxter to have the last word. At the end of his final gubernatorial address to the 1923 session, he stated, no doubt with a twinkle in his eye:

"But when your granddaughters and great-granddaughters are sitting here legislating for the State of Maine and this one man whom I am speaking of is surrounded by them, I am sure they will treat him with the same courtesies and kindliness with which you have treated Mrs. Pinkham."

☙

8.23 *Probably every automobile in town—and its proud owner—was lined up on Brunswick's Maine Street in 1911 for this panoramic view of the new world of personal mobility.*

8.24

❧

8.24 *Gail Laughlin, of Portland, the first*
Maine woman to practice law (1898), a
longtime member of the Maine House and
Senate, and a leader in the women's
suffrage movement.

❧ GAIL LAUGHLIN

Among the other women who blazed a trail through the masculine dominion of the Maine Legislature was Gail Laughlin of Portland, also an outspoken Republican. Her life had already been devoted, long before she first ran for the Maine House in 1929, to changing conditions and attitudes that women had to face.

She had grown up in the small Washington County town of Robbinston, then moved to Portland, where she saved enough money working as a secretary to pay her way through Wellesley College. Upon graduation, she announced—to the dismay of her mother, for whom college meant access to an appropriate husband—that she wanted to become a lawyer. Accepted finally at Cornell Law School, she was one of three women in a class of 123. Her fellow students began to take her seriously when she became captain of the debating team. In 1898, she passed the bar as one of the first female attorneys in the country, and by 1902 she was employed as counsel by the National American Woman Suffrage Association. Her travels for the NAWSA often took her to the west, where suffrage had been granted already in Wyoming, Colorado, Idaho, and Utah. She settled in Denver, then in San Francisco. Suddenly, she grew homesick for Maine and returned to Portland. Women now had the vote nationwide, but Gail Laughlin's vision was wider. She wanted full equal rights, and she wanted them enshrined in an Equal Rights Amendment to the U.S. Constitution. In pursuit of that goal, she once actually drove to South Dakota to present the idea to President Calvin Coolidge, who was there inaugurating Mount Rushmore.

Her work in the Maine Legislature (she served three terms in the House and three terms in the Senate) covered a broader range of issues than merely the problems of women, although she certainly zeroed in on those that came to her attention, like fighting a law that would allow girls to marry as young as 13, or changing the rules of commitment of the insane to penalize false testimony from husbands bent on incarcerating their wives. With the advent of the New Deal, she attacked the National Recovery Act for loo practices unfair to women. She was also an early environmentalist, a foe of billboards, who helped preserve a bird sanctuary in Portland's Back Cove. When a plan for a national forest in Washington County was opposed by the paper companies, she supported it because local people, hurt by the Depression, wanted to be able to sell their land to the government. She also fought for uniform lobster measures, a minimum wage, and a limit on working hours in fish packing plants.

In her later years, after leaving the Legislature, she worked as the Reporter of Court Decisions, a state post to which Governor Sumner Sewall appointed her. Gail Laughlin died in March 1952, a woman ahead of her time in the struggle for full equal rights for her sex.

By 1973, Laughlin's dream of constitutional protection for women had come true—at least to the extent that Congress had approved an Equal Rights Amendment (ERA), and it was now up to the states to ratify it. Dire predictions were made about the relations between the sexes if the amendment were to pass, even to the claim that there

8.25

∿

8.25 *The well appointed interior of Portland's now demolished Union Station evokes the great age of travel by rail.*

would have to be unisex bathrooms. Some of the most ferocious opponents were women themselves, some of whom argued that they had not needed an ERA to get ahead. Benjamin Dorsky, the venerable head of the AFL-CIO, at first opposed ratification, asserting that it would take away hard-won privileges for women workers. An outcry from the female members of his unions soon had him reversing his position. The bill passed in the Maine House but died in the Senate by one vote. The following year, it was passed by both bodies, and Maine joined the ranks of the ratifying states, which, however, did not reach the required three-fourths majority. Gail Laughlin's dream still remains a dream.

8.26

~

8.26 and 8.27 The photos may have been posed, but the work was in earnest as Bath authorities seized illegal alcohol, in these 1926 (facing page) and 1931 raids. Maine's lonely, irregular coast has long been a haven for smugglers.

~ NATIONAL PROHIBITION

Neal Dow would have been ecstatic. In 1919, the 18th Amendment to the U.S. Constitution was ratified and henceforward the prohibitionist dream of a nationwide Maine Law forbidding the sale and consumption of alcoholic beverages was a reality. So, too, were many of the problems associated with Prohibition—problems that Maine had been experiencing for decades. Enforcement of the law, of course, was always the primary challenge. Suppliers were ever on hand to quench the thirst of millions of otherwise law-abiding citizens, eager for a drink. National Prohibition increased the intensity of the difficulties in Maine because of the state's proximity to Canada, where the sale of alcoholic beverages was legal and smugglers were operating en masse.

In 1924, President Calvin Coolidge ordered a number of World War I destroyers to be taken out of mothballs, extended U.S. jurisdiction 12 miles out to sea, and scattered a "Rum Row" of liquor supply ships that had been anchored beyond the three-mile limit off New York, Boston, and other major ports. An unintended consequence was to make the overland route from Canada through Maine all the more attractive.

There was a certain irony in this outcome, for the suggestgion that naval destroyers be used in liquor enforcement had come from none other than Maine's teetotalling Governor, Percival Baxter.

At the 1923 National Governors' Conference, Baxter had garnered national headlines by stating, as reported in the *Cincinnatti Inquirer:*

Maine Chief Asserts Two Fast

Destroyers Could Put An

End To Liquor Smuggling

On Coast

Baxter also apparently said with a certain amount of smugness that Maine was doing a good job of enforcement; the trouble was that only the Federal government could stop the smuggling from Canada.

Back home, Baxter was attacked by the *Lewiston Sun,* which claimed he had not been as tough on illegal drinking as he claimed. As if to prove them wrong, Baxter publicly took on the Sheriff of Hancock County, where the problem seemed to be the worst, and tried to remove him from office.

Bar Harbor, with its wealthy socialites willing to pay well for contraband "hooch," was a hotbed of almost wide open smuggling. A local bootlegger, Daniel Herlihy, earned enough money to buy an estate and live, Gatsby-like, among them—until he was finally convicted by the U.S. Attorney and landed in a Federal prison. The Sheriff, Ward W. Westcott, a Republican stalwart and four term veteran, was known for looking the other way.

Despite Westcott's party credentials, Baxter hauled him to Augusta for a trial before the Executive Council. Witness after witness told of observing frequent liquor runs while complaisant deputies paid no attention. However, Baxter lost the battle when the Council, except for one member (Baxter's half-brother Rupert), voted to acquit the Sheriff.

Not long afterward, a far more serious scandal erupted in Aroostook County. Several leading citizens of Houlton were arrested for liquor smuggling, including the Sheriff. This time, Baxter received the resignation he demanded and the Sheriff was sent to the Atlanta Penitentiary.

In Aroostook County, smuggling gangs that were a pale imitation of the mobsters of Chicago raced about in speeding cars or, as one unfortunate resident tried, dragging a sledgeload of booze, from which, when he tried to escape the authorities, he was shot and killed. Although they never achieved the reputation of an Al Capone, some of these lawbreakers were locally famous. Joe Walnut was probably the most notorious. His real name was Albenie J. Violette. He owned hotels on both sides of the border, controlled bottling plants, the largest, most modern distillery in New Brunswick, had a fleet of vehicles, paid off inspectors and judges, and even made his nephew the police chief in his home town of Van Buren.

The nation's experiment with Prohibition was brief and unhappy and ended with the ratification of the 21st Amendment in 1933. That action effectively terminated Maine's far longer experiment of trying to ban the consumption of liquor. For almost 100 years, the issue had been at the center of Maine politics and, since the 1850s, had helped sustain the lengthy domination of the Republican Party. The demise of Prohibition as a burning public concern coincided with the election to the presidency of Franklin Delano Roosevelt. Maine, too, despite its being one of only two states to vote against FDR in 1936, would reflect the significant change that swept over the United States with his coming to power.

8.27

8.28

8.29

∾

8.28, 8.29 and 8.30 Working for the Maine

Development Commission from 1936 to

1955, photographer George French documented

the state's economy in photos such as these of

potato farming in Arroostook County,

blueberry processing in Washington County,

and lobstering.

∾ **THE NEW DEAL**

Campobello Island is not part of Maine. Today, a short bridge connects this island where the young Franklin Delano Roosevelt spent his summers to the Maine town of Lubec. Elected on the promise of restoring the country's Depression ravaged economy, Roosevelt knew Down East Maine very well.

In July 1933, he received two visitors from Washington County at the White House, Moses B. Pike, of a family long influential in the Eastport area, and Dexter Cooper, an engineer who was a neighbor of the Roosevelts on Campobello.

Back in 1920, Cooper had talked to FDR about his pet project of harnessing the huge tides in Passamaquoddy Bay in order to generate low priced electricity. That year, FDR was running for Vice-President and publicly endorsed the idea while campaigning—at least in Eastport. With the New Deal in 1933 actively pushing for economic growth, the Quoddy project seemed a natural. Two months after their visit, Pike and Cooper were applying to the Public Works Administration (PWA) for a $43 million loan.

Cooper had experienced many vicissitudes in trying to promote his dream. Attacks by opponents, some of whom objected to public power generation and others who saw Quoddy as a huge waste of money, were unrelenting during the 1920s and, despite FDR's support, continued their resistance during his presidency. The Federal Power Commission called Quoddy unsound financially, and the PWA rejected the loan application.

Stubborn as ever, Cooper and his Maine supporters, who included Governor Louis Brann—Maine's first Democratic chief executive to serve two terms since before the Civil War—continued to fight for Quoddy. A new study, supervised by Kenneth Sills, president of Bowdoin College, gave the project better financial marks. The PWA was persuaded by Interior Secretary Harold J. Ickes to reverse its decision, and it came up with $30 million to fund a scaled down version restricted to the American side of the bay.

8.30

Army engineers began to build a housing site for the workers who would erect the dam. Those buildings, dubbed Quoddy Village, still exist. For a brief time, the area around Eastport bustled with the activity of 5,000 workers. But in Congress, opponents caught up with the project, repeating their cries of boondoggle. FDR did not put up a battle when the House Appropriations Committee dropped Quoddy's funding from their bill. Dexter Cooper died. And so did Quoddy. An attempt to revive it during the Kennedy administration was brief and unsuccessful.

8.31

Nonetheless, FDR's "alphabet soup"—the initialed agencies that burst on the scene during the fevered first hundred days after his election (e.g., WPA, NRA, PWA, NLRB, and CCC)—had a lasting impact on Maine. The Civilian Conservation Corps, at least in terms of sentimentality, may have left the strongest mark. In 1985, those young men who had toiled in the Maine woods half a century earlier flocked together for a nostalgia filled reunion. The CCC had been one of the earliest New Deal measures, coming into existence less than a month after FDR took office. Its tenure in Maine involved 20,434 individuals and the pouring of $22 million into the state's economy.

From Alfred in the south to Patten and Princeton in the north, camps were created and stocked with unemployed young men, not all of them from Maine. For many of those who came from the big cities, it was their first time in the woods. The emphasis was on forestry work and included insect control, averting forest fire danger, and constructing trails, roads, and bridges in the wilderness. The Maine CCC camps spent a total of 30,000 man days in fire suppression and 2,000 man days in patrolling fire lines, pulled out millions of wild currant and gooseberry bushes (which harbor the white pine blister rust), helped complete the Maine portion of the Appalachian Trail, and carved eleven miles of road through a remote corner of the White Mountain National Forest.

8.32

8.33

8.31 *(facing page) Franco-American workers on strike, Portland, 1937. As far back as the 1860s, portions of Maine's labor force had organized to fight for decent wages and safer working conditions. The struggle was not won, however, until federal labor legislation was passed as part of the New Deal.*

8.32 *This parade float in Bangor in the 1920s serves as a reminder that since colonial times Maine has had a small black community, many of its members descendants of 18th and 19th-century sailors and stevedores.*

8.33 *Admiral Donald MacMillan demonstrated his dog team in wintry downtown Portland in 1924, evidence of the fascination with Arctic exploration in the early 20th-century. A Mainer, after all, had discovered the North Pole—Admiral Robert Peary, in 1909.*

8.34

8.34 The Fidelity Building (1910), as depicted in a promotional brochure for Portland in 1923. Despite its Beaux Arts trim, this ten-story structure on Monument Square was the first modern skyscraper in Maine.

The late Bill Clark, a popular Maine author and newspaper columnist, never forgot his experience in the CCC. In later years, Clark was an ultraconservative politically, frequently railing against government spending and "hand-outs." Yet the CCC always had his approval. He was able to see it as an investment. Maybe, in Clark's mind, it was also an example of where government red tape could be of unexpected service to an individual. Clark had never been admitted to the CCC but took the place of a local man who had been hired to teach Bronx children how to use an ax. At pay day, after a month, Clark had to admit that his last name was not Joyce. The CCC officers thought of the endless paper work this discovery would cause if it were revealed, so they agreed to cover for him.

The Captain barked: "All right, you stupid jughead, we're going to let you stay. But remember, damn it, if Joyce dies, we'll have to bury you."

∾ LABOR TROUBLES

The Roosevelt era saw the coming of age of the American labor union movement. The absence of an actively hostile President in the White House made a real difference. But until the passage of the National Labor Relations Act (Wagner Act) and the upholding of its constitutionality by the Supreme Court in 1937, there was tension enough on the labor scene to cause violence, even in normally peaceable Maine.

There had been unions in Maine since before the turn of the century. One of the earliest, surprisingly, was the "Lobster Fishermen's National Protective Association," which by 1907 had

8.35

∾

8.35 *L.L. Bean's catalogues carried an image of*

Maine as an unspoiled fishing and hunting

paradise across the world.

∾

8.36 *Company founder Leon Leonwood Bean shows*

a customer a pair of the famous Maine hunting

shoes in his Freeport sporting goods store. Founded

in 1912, L. L. Bean and Maine soon became

synonymous in the minds of many hunters,

fishermen, and campers.

8.37

8.38

8.39

8.37 *(facing page) World War II disrupted the lives of virtually every Mainer but proved a stimulus for the state's defense industries. News bulletins in downtown Portland, 1939.*

8.38 *(facing page) A female welder at a Maine shipyard, 1942.*

8.39 *Jubilant crowds celebrating V-J Day in Monument Square, 1945.*

8.40 *Jan Marinus Domela*, Monhegan

Island, 1938. *The remote fishing community*

of Monhegan became a favorite subject for a

number of 20th-century painters, who saw

such islands as refuges from the upheavals of

the Depression and the war.

managed to enroll 1,055 members in 22 locals among this group of rugged individualists. But, in Republican Maine, union organizing did not usually find fruitful ground, even after FDR swept into office and Democrat Louis Brann held onto the Governor's seat for a pair of successive terms.

The worst instance of labor violence in Maine occurred in 1937. Nationally, labor had split when the feisty young Congress of Industrial Organizations (CIO) broke away from the American Federation of Labor (AF of L). The break hit home in Maine when the Textile Workers Union, expelled from the AF of L, joined the CIO. An aggressive CIO organizing team began trying to line up workers at the 19 shoe "shops" or factories in the Lewiston-Auburn area. Thwarted by management from joining a union, the employees went on strike and then grew outraged at a local judge's injunction against their staying out of work. More than 1,000 angry workers marched over the bridge from Lewiston into Auburn and were met by state troopers and local police. Tear gas and flailing clubs repulsed them. Charging again, they flung rocks. An officer was knocked unconscious. Following a second retreat of the workers, National Guardsmen were brought in and patrolled Auburn with fixed bayonets. The Wagner Act' eventually forced the shoe shop owners to allow organizing in their factories, with the outcome of representation dependent on a majority vote.

The year 1937 also saw the election to the presidency of the Maine AF of L of the man who was to give the state's labor movement the stability it needed to mature. Benjamin J. Dorsky of Bangor was a movie picture projectionist turned organizer. For many years he headed his own organization and later the combined AFL-CIO. Although Maine never became as unionized as many other industrial states, Ben Dorsky helped make organized labor a respectable force on the Maine public scene, especially after World War II started and the war effort transformed the Maine economy.

∾ WORLD WAR II

Beginning in 1941, Maine's contribution to the war effort—in addition to the thousands of servicemen and women who left its borders—lay mainly in its production capacity. Shipyards at Bath, South Portland, and Kittery geared up for an output of surface ships and submarines dwarfing in numbers any previous efforts. The ships rolled out—83 destroyers in Bath, alone, and 274 Liberty ships and

8.40

8.41

other freighters at the yards that the same company, Bath Iron Works, constructed in South Portland. Of the total of American Liberty ships, 10 percent were built at South Portland. A workforce of fewer than 2,000 in 1939 expanded to more than 12,000 by 1943.

Kittery fabricated 85 submarines between 1939 and 1945. The workforce there ballooned to 20,000. On one day in January 1944, four subs were launched. The sub overhaul work that is now the specialty of the yard was also started in World War II, when 74 vessels were worked on.

New military facilities were also created in Maine. A county fairgrounds in Aroostook County was turned into a major military airfield at Presque Isle. Bangor's Dow Field found itself transformed into a vital transit point for American aircraft flying to Europe. To patrol for enemy U-boats off the coast, a small local airfield was turned into the Brunswick Naval Air Station.

During World War I, the Germans had infiltrated a saboteur into northern Maine whose mission was to blow up the railroad bridge at Vanceboro linking Maine and New Brunswick, Canada. Not wanting to be shot as a spy, he dressed himself up in full uniform and, as such, was apprehended by the Sheriff of Washington County before he could set off his charges.

A less slapstick infiltration occurred during World War II. Two German spies were landed at Hancock Point

8.42

8.43

≈

in November 1944. They hid their rubber raft and, suitcases in hand, made their way to Route 1. En route, they were spotted by a high school boy driving home from a dance who reported his suspicions to his father, a Hancock County Deputy Sheriff. When the rubber boat was found, the local authorities called in the FBI. The two Germans were allowed to reach New York City, where they were taken into custody.

Far more German belligerents entered Maine during the war, but as prisoners. A prisoner of war camp in Houlton held many of them, and some were pressed into service as pulp cutters for the Great Northern Paper Company.

When the atom bomb was dropped on Hiroshima in 1945, Maine's Governor Horace Hildreth had just called a conference to discuss what to do about the veterans who would soon be coming home. At least 15,000 had already returned, and 3,000 of these were unemployed. From Washington came the good news, via Senator Margaret Chase Smith, that Dow Field would stay open.

8.41 *(facing page) The end of World War II meant a return to normal life for most citizens of the state.*

A time honored domestic art, c. 1950.

≈

8.42 *A new way of putting dinner on the table, 1955.*

≈

8.43 *Welcoming home Dad, 1951.*

9.1

THE PAST HALF CENTURY

❧ POST-WAR REALITIES

V J DAY WAS CELEBRATED IN MAINE with as much enthusiasm as anywhere else in the United States. People rode on the roofs of jam-packed cars circling through Bangor; bonfires burned in the streets of Portland, while soldiers and civilians hoisted an effigy of Hirohito onto the statue in Monument Square; Biddeford's town hall plaza filled with dancing couples; the South Portland shipyards blasted their whistles continuously, and a dynamite blast set off on Vinalhaven broke 100 windows.

When the parties were over, there was a sense that once more Maine had reached a watershed and that the Pine Tree State would never be the same again.

The full extent of the change was not immediately apparent. The veterans continued to come home. The Republican Party continued to dominate Maine politics, projecting an image of steady solidity to some and mossback conservatism to others. The paper and power companies still wielded great influence. Agriculture played an important part in the state's economy, as did the cheap labor employed in many of the factories, particularly those producing shoes and textiles. In 1947, two years after the war's end, potato production in Aroostook County reached its peak. That same year, construction began on the Maine Turnpike, one of the first of the "superhighways" in the U.S. and, to an extent unanticipated at the time, a major contributor to economic development. The tensions of the cold war in the 1950s brought military expenditures flooding into Maine; although Presque Isle and Dow were closed, the Loring Strategic Air Command Base in Limestone was created, and millions of dollars spent on the Brunswick Naval Air Station, Bath Iron Works, the Portsmouth Naval Shipyard in Kittery, and other Defense Department contractors. The late 1960s saw the peak of the shoe industry, which had filled the vacuum left when textile manufacturing had been lured to the South by even

❧

9.1 *Andrew Wyeth,* Bridge at Martinsville (Morris Cove), *1939. Wyeth's oils and watercolors of the countryside near Cushing—notably* Christina's World—*are perhaps the most widely known images of rural coastal Maine in this century.*

9.2

9.3

cheaper labor than in Maine. Then, foreign competition started to hurt the lower end priced shoes made in Maine. During the 1980s, shoe "shops" closed all over Maine. The same thing happened to another Maine industry that relied on low wages: large-scale poultry farming.

∾ EDMUND S. MUSKIE

A survey of the Maine political scene in 1954 could never have predicted that one day the University of Southern Maine would have an Edmund S. Muskie Institute of Public Affairs, named for a man who became Governor, U.S. Senator, and U.S. Secretary of State, and who was a candidate for Vice-President and President.

For Ed Muskie was a Democrat, and in 1954 the Maine Democratic Party had seemingly reached the nadir of its post-Civil War fortunes in the Pine Tree State. There was not a single Democrat in statewide or congressional office. The previous Legislature had only two Democratic State Senators opposing 33 Republicans and a mere 24 House Democrats as against 127 Republicans. The minority party could not even exert the power of blocking an emergency vote, which requires two-thirds of each chamber.

Muskie's run for the governorship in 1954 was to have been a warm-up for 1956. The last Democratic Governor had been Louis Brann in the early 1930s. Although he had served two consecutive terms, Brann, like the other four Democrat chief executives since the Civil War, had had no chance to build up any party strength. In most cases, their elections had been due to splits in the Republican ranks. When those splits were healed, the GOP had always easily swept back into control.

Ed Muskie did have the advantage of a Republican split in 1954. The incumbent, Governor Burton Cross, had won his party's primary in a tough campaign. One of the men he had bested, a Stockton Springs farmer named Neal Bishop, then ran against him as an independent. When Muskie faced Cross in 1954, Bishop openly supported Muskie.

Years later, Bishop would run as a Republican against incumbent U.S. Senator Muskie and be blown away. The intervening years saw a meteoric rise for the young lawyer of Polish ancestry from Rumford and Waterville. His astonishing victory in

9.4

9.2 *(facing page, above) U. S. Senator Edmund S. Muskie pauses at the famous roadsign in Lynchville, Maine, during a 1958 campaign. Muskie, who also served as U. S. Secretary of State and ran unsuccessfully for the Democratic nomination for President, was a major force behind federal clean air and clean water legislation.*

∾

9.3 *(facing page, below) Winter pastimes like skating and sledding have been popular in Maine since colonial times, but the mid 20th-century brought a new sense of speed: here is the state's first registered snowmobile, a 1966 Bombardier Ski-Doo, now in the Maine State Museum.*

∾

9.4 *Norman Rockwell's cartoons, which today hang in the State House, were commissioned in the 1950s as part of a state tourist promotion campaign.*

9.5 The demolition of Portland's chateauesque Union Station in 1961 served as a rallying cry for Maine's newly awakened historic preservation movement.

1954 drew national attention, and his performance as Governor, even given a Republican Legislature and Executive Council, helped him to gain the support he needed to defeat former Governor Frederick Payne for the U.S. Senate seat in 1958.

One of Muskie's gubernatorial achievements was a law to classify Maine's rivers, as a prelude to cleaning them up. At the time, the Androscoggin and the Penobscot were considered to be among the most polluted waterways in the country. It was his activity as a pioneer environmentalist that earned him the title, in the U.S. Senate, of "Mr. Clean." He achieved a national reputation for championing clean water, clean air, and other conservation measures in an America beginning to demand better environmental quality. In 1968, Hubert Humphrey chose Muskie to be his running mate on the presidential ticket. The favorable impression he made as a Vice Presidential candidate, although the race was lost by a narrow margin, left him in a good position to run for President four years later.

A series of "dirty tricks" in the New Hampshire primary helped undercut his campaign, particularly an incident in Manchester when he was reported to have wept in public, which was taken as a sign of "weakness" in a politician in those days. With Muskie displaced by the ultra-liberal George McGovern—possibly the Republicans' strategy—the Democrats went down to resounding defeat. Muskie remained in the U.S. Senate and capped his distinguished career by becoming the U.S. Secretary of State during the Iran hostage crisis.

∾ MARGARET CHASE SMITH

Dirty tricks were tried, too, against Margaret Chase Smith, the
first woman to serve as a U.S. Senator from Maine and, indeed,
the first woman whose name was ever put in nomination for
President by a major political party. In 1954, when she was running
for re-election, some of her opponents spread a rumor that she
had terminal cancer and had stayed in the race only so that
Governor Burton Cross could appoint himself to the seat after
they were both returned to office. As it turned out, Cross was not
even re-elected and Smith was perfectly healthy. Earlier, in the 1948
Republican U.S. Senate primary, facing three men—including two
ex-Governors whom she eventually beat—she had to deal with the
whispered rumor that she had broken up her late husband's first
marriage.

Such challenges were easily overcome by the ex-telephone
operator from Skowhegan. In that same 1954 election, she had pri-
mary opposition, instigated by Wisconsin Senator Joseph McCarthy, whose smear tactics she had
assailed in her courageous "Declaration of Conscience" speech four years earlier. McCarthy had
sworn revenge and had handpicked a candidate named Robert L. Jones to run against Smith. The
same year that the Wisconsin demagogue's career came to a crashing end, the Senator from Maine
beat back his candidate by a 5 to 1 margin.

Margaret Chase Smith had not intended to enter politics. In 1930, she married Clyde Smith, an
up-and-coming young Republican from her hometown. A rarity in Maine politics in the 1920s and
1930s, a champion of labor and of minorities like the Franco-Americans, Smith was serving in the
U.S. Congress when he died of a heart attack in 1940. His widow ran for his seat and won. Having
lectured even before the war on the need for a strong Navy, she was able to secure a place as the first
woman on the Naval Affairs Committee, an important place to be after World War II broke out.

9.6

∾

9.6 *U. S. Senator Margaret Chase Smith, famous in*
Maine for her close attention to her constituents, greets two
voters on a log boom at the St. Croix Paper Company in
Woodland in 1960. Smith earned national fame as the first
woman to serve in both houses of Congress and for her
"Declaration of Conscience," written in her Skowhegan
kitchen, a rejection of the demagogic tactics of her fellow
Republican, Senator Joseph McCarthy.

9.7

9.7 The Maine Turnpike—and not long afterwards, Interstate 95—linked Maine's tourist and industrial economy with the rest of New England.

During her career in the U.S. Senate, Margaret Chase Smith became known for three things: she wore a red rose every day, she never missed a roll call vote and she was not afraid to speak her mind, as evidenced by her attack on McCarthy at a time when almost every politician in the country was afraid of being labelled a "Communist" by him.

In 1964, she made a serious run for the presidency, entering primaries in New Hampshire, Illinois and Oregon. In Illinois, she captured 30 percent of the vote and arrived at the GOP convention with 16 delegates. Senator George Aiken of Vermont placed her name in nomination—a first at a major party conclave—and she received 27 votes while Barry Goldwater was winning the nomination.

When she ran for a fourth term in 1972, her age had become a factor, and she was defeated by the Democratic Congressman from the Second District, William Hathaway. In 1989, she was honored with the nation's highest civilian award, the Medal of Freedom. She retired to her native Skowhegan, where the Margaret Chase Smith Library, containing her papers, had been established, and where she died, aged 97, in 1995.

9.8

9.8 *This study of John Marin at Cape Split in 1951 by photographer George Daniell expresses what drew the painter to Maine: the confrontation of a Modernist sensibility with the power of water, rocks, and sky. Marin shared with Hartley the rejection of the notion that Modernism is solely an urban phenomenon.*

9.9

ꙮ THE BIG PROJECTS

Virtually every Governor since 1851 had been promising to bring jobs to Maine and to do it with spectacular projects. Developments on a grand scale had happened: i.e., John A. Poor's successful effort to bring in the Grand Trunk Railroad, the creation of Millinocket by the Great Northern Paper Company, and huge hydroelectric projects like the Central Maine Power Company's Wyman Dam on the upper Kennebec.

But in the later decades of the 20th-century, such massive attempts to industrialize Maine more thoroughly met with strong resistance. The Quoddy project for harnessing the powerful tides Down East was eventually defeated. A good deal of the objection to Quoddy had been based on the fact that, like the Tennessee Valley Authority, it would have been run by the Federal government and would have sold power in competition with private utilities. What finally shot Quoddy down in the early 1960s was that its cost/benefit ratio was unfavorable—in other words, it would cost more to build than the power was worth. Its supporters then tried to link it with another proposed power project on the St. John River at a site known as Dickey-Lincoln School.

Quoddy and Dickey-Lincoln failed to make it as a package. But some people, particularly in Aroostook County, felt that Dickey-Lincoln could stand on its own as a power generating project that would bring industrialization and prosperity to their poor and isolated section of the state. Previous opponents of such ideas had been mostly conservative businessmen, especially utility executives unhappy about government investment. Now, they had new allies—the environmentalists.

9.10

9.9 (facing page) Maine Yankee Nuclear Power Plant, Wiscasset, went on line in 1972. Despite vigorous referendum campaigns in the 1980s and early 1990s to shut it down, the majority of Maine voters endorsed nuclear power as an energy source.

9.10 Whitewater rafting on the Kennebec at Harris Hydroelectric Station. In 1976, enthusiasts for the sport discovered that the daily release of water from the dam each summer—up to 8,000 cubic feet per second—provided a thrilling ride through the twelve miles of the Kennebec Gorge.

9.11

∾

9.11 *The Belgian born writer Marguerite Yourcenar, who*

became in 1980 the first woman to be elected to the French

Academy, lived from 1950 on in Northeast Harbor, where

she completed one of the great novels of the century, The

Memoirs of Hadrian *(1951).*

Originally, Dickey-Lincoln was promoted as an "environmentalist's dam." Two previous proposals for dams on the St. John would have flooded the Allagash wilderness. Some of the same supporters of Dickey-Lincoln pushed through a bill in the 1964-66 Maine Legislature, which was dominated by Democrats after President Lyndon Johnson's landslide, that created an Allagash Wilderness Waterway, forever preserving almost 23,000 acres of land and 30,000 acres of pristine water in the Allagash watershed.

So Dickey-Lincoln was left as the only show in town. All of Maine's political leaders were for it in a bipartisan effort that lasted until 1975. Then, with environmental concerns growing nationwide, Second District Congressman and later U.S. Senator William Cohen changed his position and opposed the dam. Maneuvers to keep Dickey and then Lincoln School alive continued until 1983, when the House Public Works Committee voted to de-authorize the project.

Another grandiose plan for boosting the economy of Aroostook County also had strong bipartisan support at the outset. This was a move to diversify the county's agricultural mainstay of potatoes by adding a sugar beet crop. In the past, sugar beets had been grown in Maine, but never commercialized to the extent envisaged in the scheme brought forward by a potato processor from New Jersey named Fred H. Vahlsing. He was to build a $14.5 million sugar refinery and add hundreds of jobs to a region significantly losing population. Senators Muskie and Smith went to bat and procured an allotment from Congress of 33,000 acres. The Republican Governor, John H. Reed (himself an Aroostook potato farmer) and a Democratic Legislature then passed a controversial bill on which, said Vahlsing, the entire future of the project rested. He needed to lower the water quality classification of a small body of water, the Prestile Stream, into which he was dumping potato refuse and into which the effluent from the sugar refinery would also flow. Despite a statewide outcry, the pollution was permitted, the refinery built, and thousands of Aroostook acres planted to beets. But not really enough acres. When Vahlsing was slow about paying the farmers, production ceased, and the project collapsed. The state and Federal government, which had backed it with loan guarantees, suffered large losses, and the political recriminations continued for years. More recently, broccoli has become a successful second crop in Aroostook County.

Oil refineries proposed for the Down East coast caused just as much of a ruckus as public power and sugar beets. The nearness of deep water to shore along the coast of Washington County was the basis for believing sites there to be ideal for docking the huge supertankers then coming into use. Both Eastport and Machiasport were considered as locations for mammoth facilities of this sort. The reaction from various groups, particularly fishermen and summer residents, was one of fierce opposition, fueled by fears of massive oil spills. In the end, after stormy hearings and even a legislative attempt to zone the entire Maine coast, nothing happened. The same has been true of other major industrial projects proposed for the coastal area, such as an aluminum smelter at

9.12

Trenton near Acadia National Park and a coal-fired power plant defeated at Bucksport. The one remaining project, development of a deep water port at Sears Island, still has not been allowed to proceed after many years of litigation.

∞ THE CURTIS REVOLUTION

The development schemes of oil refineries and aluminum smelters came to the fore during the eight-year adminstration of Governor Kenneth M. Curtis who, when he took office after the election of 1966, was the youngest chief executive in the nation. For tradition-minded Maine to have elected a 35-year-old Democrat with a progressive, activist platform portended a revolution of sorts. As it turned out, the large-scale economic development projects near and dear to Ken Curtis, who had been a U.S. Department of Commerce redevelopment official in northern Maine, were not the aspect of change

∞

9.12 *The discovery in the 1980s that the Japanese would pay high prices for sea urchin roe created a new source of income for those following Maine's long tradition of seeking a living from the sea. By the 1990s, however, over-fishing of sea urchin, haddock and cod had clouded the fishing industry's future.*

9.13

∾

9.13 *Writer Stephen King, a Bangor resident,*
is another Mainer with international name
recognition. Many of his novels and stories of
the supernatural are set in rural Maine.

for which his terms in office became best known. In fact, the key elements were his environmental record, his governmental reorganization record, and, above all, his revamping of the state's tax system.

The political composition of the electorate in Maine had been slowly transforming itself since the breakthrough election of Ed Muskie in 1954. Muskie's immediate successor, Clinton Clausen, was a Democrat, too, but he had died after only a year in office. It was his Republican successor, John H. Reed, the Aroostook potato farmer, whom Curtis beat handily in 1966. Although throughout his eight years the Legislature was still controlled by Republicans, the Democrats continued to build their strength under Curtis and eventually became the majority party in the state.

The institution of a state income tax was the political act of courage for which Curtis is best known. Most Governors do not even dare to raise a tax, never mind impose an entirely new one. Curtis did both—and survived politically—but only by a handful of votes when he ran for re-election in 1970. The next year, an attempt through a citizen petition and statewide vote to repeal the income tax was repulsed far more easily. Defying all political pundits, Maine people, convinced of its fairness, voted to keep the tax by a 3 to 1 margin.

Other notable landmarks during the Curtis years were the passage of two environmental bills deemed the first of their kind in the U.S.—the Site Selection Law, which required major development projects to undergo review and receive the consent of a special Board of Environmental Protection composed of appointed citizens, and the Oil Conveyance Law, which placed a special tax on every gallon of oil transported into the state, creating a fund to deal with oil spills. Despite coastal Mainers' horror of oil spills, Portland had become the second largest oil port on the East Coast because all of the oil for Montreal is landed there and piped overland. A massive reorganization of state government was also undertaken by Curtis, reducing more than 200 separate governmental bodies into fifteen umbrella departments. A similar consolidation into a single system of the scattered University of Maine campuses was also achieved.

After leaving office, Ken Curtis served for a time as Chairman of the Democratic National Committee, U.S. Ambassador to Canada and, most recently, as president of his alma mater, the Maine Maritime Academy.

∽ THE INDEPENDENT GOVERNOR

Maine politics can be very unpredictable. Having sprung a surprise by choosing a young, liberal Democrat to run the state, the voters in 1974 selected a political neophyte of conservative bent to succeed him—and one who belonged to no political party. A Lewiston insurance executive, James B. Longley, beat both the Republican and Democratic candidates in an upset.

Longley had caught the public eye once his ex-Portland Law School classmate Governor Curtis had appointed him to head a Management and Cost Survey Commission, a group of volunteer businessmen given the task of examining state government and recommending "business-like" efficiencies to make it run better.

9.14

∽

9.14 *May Sarton (left), who spent much of her life in York, wrote movingly of old age and of the Maine coast in her journals, novels, and poetry.*

The Longley Report, when it came out, was highly controversial. Many of its proposals were unrealistic, the savings exaggerated, or the political obstacles to their achievement insuperable. After the Legislature rejected two-thirds of the recommendations, Longley had an issue to take to the people. He claimed that if he were given a free hand, he could save the taxpayers $250 million. He also boasted that he would need only one term in office to straighten everything out in Augusta. Longley was a master salesman. In insurance, he had reached the highest bracket of his trade, the Million Dollar Roundtable. With his hypnotic blue eyes and gift of gab, he went out and sold the Maine electorate. A weak Republican candidate and bruised feelings left over from a Democratic primary helped him solidify his support.

Governing without a party was an interesting feat. His term was one of the stormiest on record as he fought with both the Republicans, who controlled the State Senate, and the Democrats, who controlled the House. No Governor since Percival Baxter vetoed as many bills. Most of them were overridden, often by enormous margins and even unanimously. In a famous incident, he prompted a shouting match over dinner with the legislative leadership at the Blaine House when he referred to legislators as "pimps."

Yet Jim Longley remained extremely popular. He might have been re-elected had he chosen to run again, but he had said he would only serve one term, and he kept his word.

One thing he hadn't been able to do was to broaden his support. In the 1976 legislative elections at his midterm, a number of his followers (dubbed "Longley's Legions") ran as Independent candidates, including his own sister. Not one of them was elected.

A few months following his retirement from office, he was on a skiing trip with his family when he suddenly felt a tremendous pain in his stomach, "like a horse kicked me," he said. The trouble was diagnosed as stomach cancer. Within a few months, James B. Longley was dead at the age of 50.

∾ THE INDIAN LAND CLAIMS CASE

It was during Longley's term as Governor that the distant past caught up with Maine in the shape of the Indian Land Claims Case. For a period of time, at least two-thirds of Maine was subject to a legal claim upon it by two Indian tribes—the Penobscots and the Passamaquoddies—still in existence.

In the course of researching a dispute between the Passamaquoddies and a non-Indian trying to bulldoze a road through their property, a young law student named Tom Tureen discovered that in 1790 the U.S. Congress had passed a law called the Indian Non-Intercourse Act and requiring all treaties henceforth negotiated between states and Indian tribes to be ratified by Congress. The treaties signed with the Penobscots and Passamaquoddies by Massachusetts (of which Maine was then a part) had both occurred after 1790 and had never been submitted to Congress. Since it was through these treaties that the tribes had given up millions of acres of land and since they were now legally null and void, the titles to those lands were suddenly under a cloud.

In 1975, a higher court upheld the contention of Federal District Judge Edward T. Gignoux that the Non-Intercourse Act applied to Maine's Indians. Governor Longley adamantly refused to concede that the Indians' claim had merit. In this, he was backed by the Attorney General, Democrat Joseph

9.15 *The Allagash "beauty strip," a narrow band of real forest amid the "industrial" forest and clear cuts typical of central and northern Maine in the late 20th-century.*

9.15

Brennan, who was later to succeed Longley as Governor. The crisis reached full bloom when Ropes and Gray, the prestigious Boston bond counsel, declared they could not give unqualified approval to municipal bond sales in the area the tribes claimed and a $27 million issue had to be cancelled.

The Indians had been asking for $150 million, which Tom Tureen, now representing them, pointed out was only for the loss of rent on their lands. The real cost of idemnifying them would be $25 billion!

Attempts to work out a compromise were begun after Maine's Congressional delegation was unable to pass legislation to extinguish the Indians' claim. President Jimmy Carter appointed a Georgia Supreme Court Justice, William Gunter, to try to work out a settlement. The initial proposal called for a payment of $25 million to the two tribes, a grant of 300,000 acres, and the option to buy 200,000

9.16

more. Angry opposition from Longley, Brennan, and the two Republican Congressmen, William Cohen and David Emery, was matched by the support for a compromise from Democratic U.S. Senators Muskie and William Hathaway. In the end, although Hathaway was defeated for re-election by Cohen, an agreement was reached. The Indians actually received more money, $81.5 million, and the right to use some of it to buy up to 300,000 acres of land.

∾ ENVIRONMENTAL POLITICS

Earth Day was first promoted in 1970, but throughout the postwar years the debate of "payrolls versus pickerel" had intensified. Plans to bring oil refineries, tanker docks, aluminum smelters, and giant dams to the state met determined opposition. The state government adopted a "Site Selection Law," the first of its kind in the country, which allowed regulation of large-scale industrial sites. In 1963, a major wild river in far northern Maine, the Allagash, was declared off-limits to total development by logging companies, and a narrow corridor on both banks was set aside as the Allagash Wilderness Waterway. The vast Maine woods, an "industrial" forest administered as the state's "unoccupied territories" for schooling and taxation purposes, was subjected to zoning when the Land Use Regulation Commission was formed. The state's major rivers, which had been turned into open sewers for domestic waste and industrial chemicals, were finally cleaned up through an expensive sewage treatment campaign and strict regulations on dumping pollutants into them. Although the paper companies threatened to leave Maine, they stayed, learned they could save money by reusing their chemicals, and, in some cases, even expanded their operations.

The spillover from the electronics companies along Route 128 near Boston also reached Maine. Companies like Fairchild Semiconductor and Digital located plants here, taking advantage of a labor force whose wages were still not exhorbitant and whose work ethic was exemplary. The growth in such businesses and the success of small entrepreneurs brought opportunities for venture capital, as did interstate banking. Tourism and the real estate market expanded to the point where a backlash was created, with communities trying to restrict development. It was a far cry from the days after World War II when thousands of young people were leaving the state. In the 1980s, new people were coming to

9.17

9.16 (facing page) Established in 1916 by rich summer residents on Mount Desert Island who wanted to preserve a retreat from the urban, industrial world, Acadia National Park by the late 20th-century had become a crowded tourist attraction, the most popular national park east of the Rockies.

9.17 Late 20th-century ski resorts like Sugarloaf in the Carrabassett Valley, whose miles of trails are shown on the map, and Sunday River in Bethel helped make "vacationland" a year-round experience.

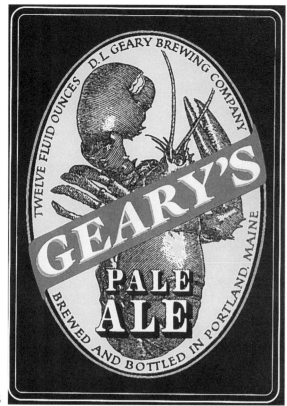

9.18

~

9.18 *Neal Dow would have been horrified, but one of the marketing successes of the 1990s was the popularity of the state's new micro-brewery beers, many of which drew on Maine images and place names in selling their product.*

live in Maine, often drawn by its much envied "quality of life." Loss of population was turned into a surplus as Maine went over the one million mark. The state's budget surplus of $2.5 million in 1983 reached $100 million in 1988. A Growth Management Act was a high priority for the Legislature that passed it, incorporating the fears of many that development was out of control. It was a period when unemployment in Maine stood at the incredibly low figure of 2.9 percent.

The recession of the 1990s burst this balloon, and Maine once more is scrambling to recover. In-migration has slowed if not altogether halted. The collapse of the real estate boom in southern Maine has had a severe impact. The state government's surplus fell to back-to-back deficits of more than 30 percent. Cutbacks in defense spending have hurt some communities.

Yet the Maine that struggles to emerge from the ill-effects of the recession is a far different place from Maine at the end of World War II. As if in a reversion to an earlier day, "Maine has slowly returned to a position of being significantly involved in world trade, as it was a century ago," to quote from *Changing Maine*, a publication of the Edmund S. Muskie Institute of Public Affairs at the University of Southern Maine in Portland. A far less insular state finds itself shipping products to Japan and China, receiving aquaculture investments from Norway, depending on Canadian tourists, and having formal trade exchanges with Brazil, Russia, and Japan. The University of Maine has even set up a campus in Bulgaria. International airports at Bangor and Portland allow ease of travel to complement such arrangements.

~ MAINE IN THE GLOBAL VILLAGE

Nowhere can the merging of the old and new entity be better seen than in the metamorphosis of the mail-order and merchandising company, L. L. Bean. Started by a young Mainer who, wanting to keep his feet dry while hunting, invented a new type of rubber-and-leather boot, the sporting goods store of Leon Leonwood Bean is today a gigantic international retailer, processing 30,000 mail orders a day and also drawing thousands of visitors to its store in Freeport—which, in keeping with the policy established by L. L. Bean, stays open 24 hours a day, seven days a week, 365 days a year. Many of the company's sales and an increasing percentage of its visitors are now from overseas, and its presence in

Freeport has attracted other brand-name retailers and turned a small coastal town into a shopping mecca.

Several major strikes hit paper companies at Jay and Rumford during the 1980s, engendering a bitterness that has still not entirely dissipated in Maine's number one industry. Nuclear energy continues to be generated at the Maine Yankee plant in Wiscasset despite three failed referenda that sought to shut it down. Anger over events in Augusta led voters, through an initiated referendum, to impose consecutive term limits on the service of their legislators. Two municipal votes of note occurred over the issue of gay rights, with Portlanders upholding an ordinance to prevent discrimination against gays and lesbians and Lewiston voters repealing one. Meanwhile, the voters of Lewiston, overwhelmingly Franco-American in ethnic background, chose a black man, John Jenkins, over a Franco-American for mayor by a 3 to 1 margin. Augusta, the capital, has long had a black mayor, Bill Burney, in a state that is 99 percent white.

On the national scene, George Mitchell, the Waterville born Democrat who was favored to win the governorship in 1974 but lost to Independent James Longley, served as Majority

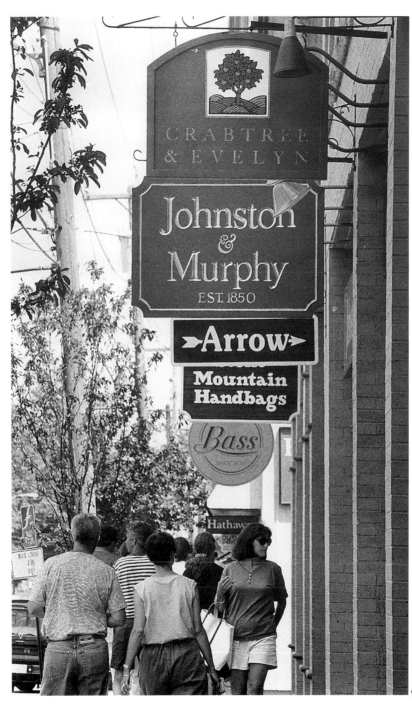

9.19

9.19 *Freeport's transformation from a quiet coastal town with a famous sporting goods store into an international discount shopping mecca was one of the economic success stories of late 20th-century Maine.*

9.20

∾

9.20   A Coastal Zone Color Scanner image

made by satellite showing chlorophyll distrib-

ution in the "garden" of the Gulf of Maine.

Microscopic plant life is a rich source of

nutrients in the food chain in Maine's waters.

Leader of the U.S. Senate from 1989 to 1994 and became one of the most powerful political figures in the country. He had left a lifetime appointment as a Federal judge when he was appointed to fill out the term of Senator Muskie, who had become Secretary of State. Most of the political pundits two years later expected that Mitchell would lose his race for re-election against a popular conservative Republican Congressman, David Emery. Yet Mitchell overcame a 36 point deficit in the polls and went on to win easily. In 1988, he was re-elected with 81 percent of the vote, but in 1994 he preferred to return to private life. His seat was won by a Republican, former Second District Congresswoman Olympia Snowe—who had recently married Brennan's successor as Governor, John R. McKernan Jr.

For four years, the state's best known summer visitor was the President of the United States, George Bush, who has vacationed at his family's home in Kennebunkport since he was a child. But President Bush failed to capture Maine in the presidential election of 1992. In fact, the Independent candidate, Ross Perot, came in second ahead of him, capturing 30 percent of the Maine vote, his best showing in the entire country.

If an important part of the "Maine mystique" has been the sheer, cussed independence of its citizens, that fact continues to hold true 175 years after Maine people demonstrated their desire to run their own affairs as a separate state. It is an interesting coincidence that Maine's current Governor—elected as an independent—bears the same family name as its first Governor William King. Rather than through shipbuilding and overseas trade, however, Governor Angus King first won public notice in the state as a political commentator on public television.

✑ THE MAINE MYSTIQUE

An identity is forged over time. And, paradoxically, time works its changes on that same identity...which is to say that Maine never really stands still. It was once characterized during an era of political stagnation as "a finished piece," a charming little miniature, embedded—to paraphrase Thomas Brackett Reed—in the liquid amber of its own folksiness.

There is still a lot of that feeling around. The bookshelves are filled with the "Sunnybrook Farm" view of Maine, with gorgeous photos of its scenic and architectural beauties, and with thin volumes of humor sporting colorful drawings of quaint characters.

But Maine, above all, is flesh and blood, real people, who may say "cute" Maine things in front of the tourists but who swear like troopers among themselves and are often very bright, rather than quaint, and full of human strengths and weaknesses. The mixture of ethnic groups, subcultures, and ideas has melded into a single yet elusive identity—the Maine "ethos," the Maine "mystique"—born out of the interaction of people with their beautiful but sometimes harsh environment.

As a separate state, Maine is marking its 175th year. It has taken from many sources, but it gives back to the nation as much, if not more, than it receives.

This is a birthday volume for the Grand Old State of Maine.

Forever "grand" and forever young.

9.21

✑

9.21 *Joan Benoit Samuelson of Freeport won the Boston Marathon while still a Bowdoin student and went on to win a gold medal in 1984 in the first Olympic women's marathon.*

ILLUSTRATION CREDITS

MSM   Maine State Museum (Augusta, ME.)
MHS   Maine Historical Society (Portland, ME.)
MHPC   Maine Historic Preservation Commission
        (Augusta, ME.)
MSA   Maine State Archives (Augusta, ME.)

DUST JACKET

Private collection

FRONTISPIECE

MSM

SECTION ONE

1.1   MSM
1.2   MSM
1.3   MSM
1.4   MSM
1.5   Robert Abbe Museum of Stone Age Antiquities
        (Bar Harbor, ME.)
1.6   MSM
1.7   MSM

SECTION TWO

2.1   MSA
2.2   Osher Map Library, University of Southern Maine
        (Portland, ME.)
2.3   Pejepscot Historical Society (Brunswick, ME.)
2.4   Royal Ontario Museum (Toronto, Canada)
2.5   Osher Map Library
2.6   Osher Map Library
2.7   The National Trust (Great Britain)
2.8   MSA
2.9   MHS
2.10   Old Fort Western (Augusta, ME.)
2.11   MSM
2.12   MSM
2.13   MHS
2.14   MSM

2.15   MHS, on loan to the MSM
2.16   Society for the Preservation of New England
        Antiquities (Boston, MA.)
2.17   MHPC
2.18   MHS
2.19   MSM
2.20   MHS

SECTION THREE

3.1   MSM
3.2   MSM
3.3   MSM
3.4   MSM
3.5   MSM
3.6   MHPC
3.7   Maine State Library (Augusta, ME.)
3.8   MSM
3.9   Bowdoin College Museum of Art (Brunswick, ME.)
3.10   MHS
3.11   MHS
3.12   MSM
3.13   MSM
3.14   MHS
3.15   MHS
3.16   Maine Humanities Council (Portland, ME.)
3.17   MHPC
3.18   Bowdoin College Museum of Art

SECTION FOUR

4.1   MSM
4.2   MSM
4.3   Pejepscot Historical Society
4.4   MSM
4.5   Farnsworth Art Museum (Rockland, ME.)
4.6   MSM
4.7   MSM
4.8   MHS
4.9   Maine State Library (Augusta, ME.)
4.10   MHS
4.11   MSM

4.12   National Gallery of Art
        (Washington, DC.)
4.13   MSM

SECTION FIVE

5.1   Private collection
5.2   MHS
5.3   MHPC
5.4   MSM
5.5   Private collection
5.6   MSM
5.7   MHS
5.8   MSM
5.9   MSM
5.10   MSM
5.11   MSM
5.12   MSM
5.13   MHS
5.14   MSM
5.15   MSM
5.16   MSM
5.17   MHS
5.18   Stowe-Day Foundation (Hartford, CT.)
5.19   MSM
5.20   MHS
5.21   MHS
5.22   MSM
5.23   MHS
5.24   MHS
5.25   MHS
5.26   MHS
5.27   MHS
5.28   MSM
5.29   MSM
5.30   MHS

SECTION SIX

6.1   MSM
6.2   MHS
6.3   MSM
6.4   Pejepscot Historical Society